THE FICTION

**DATE DUE**

WILLIAM J. PALMER

# THE FICTION
# OF JOHN FOWLES

TRADITION, ART, AND THE
LONELINESS OF SELFHOOD

A LITERARY FRONTIERS EDITION

UNIVERSITY OF MISSOURI PRESS

COLUMBIA

ACKNOWLEDGMENTS

Thanks to: Joseph Duffy, A. A. DeVitis, Janet Reed, William Epstein, Alan McKenzie, Michael Yetman, and the Purdue Research Foundation.

Excerpts from *The Collector*, *The Aristos*, *The Magus*, and *The French Lieutenant's Woman* have been quoted by permission of Anthony Sheil Associates Limited and Jonathan Cape, Inc., British publishers of the works, and of Little, Brown and Co., publishers in the United States.

The quotation from *The Myth of Sisyphus and Other Essays* by Albert Camus, translated by Justin O'Brien, Copyright 1955 has been printed by permission of Alfred A. Knopf, Inc.

The lines from T. S. Eliot's "Little Gidding" are quoted by permission of Harcourt Brace Jovanovich, Inc.

All quotations from *The Aristos* and *The French Lieutenant's Woman* are from the Signet Editions. Quotations from *The Collector* and *The Magus* are from the Dell Editions. Pages for all quotations are noted in parentheses within the text.

FOR MOM, DAD, AND MARYANN

# THE FOWLES WORLD

AN impotent kidnapper, twin actress sisters each with a double identity, Nazi sadists and an *Eleutheria* man, a Victorian prude, and a circa–1867 Soho prostitute—these are some of the characters who pace the rooms, walk the islands, and for good or bad, inhabit the world of John Fowles's fiction. The Fowles world stretches through time and space from modern-day London to the island of Phraxos off the coast of Greece to the mystic wilderness of Norway to Aix-la-Chapelle during World War I to the Dorset coast in 1867 and back to Victorian London. In the last decade, John Fowles has published three novels—two of them, *The Collector* and *The French Lieutenant's Woman*, became runaway bestsellers; the other, *The Magus*, is his most ambitious novel—and *The Aristos*, a philosophical analysis of mid-twentieth-century life. By stylistic mastery and experimental inventiveness Fowles creates worlds which can be mystical, mythical, or starkly real; or, as is most often the case, all three simultaneously.

Fowles fiction is like a huge protean amusement park, a literary Disney World enisled in a sea of potential interpretation. But the park is sinister, not gay; dark, not ferris wheel-lighted and lantern-strung. And the people who come to the park are always alone. They pass through the main gate where Dostoevsky, a microphoned Cerberus, barks, "Step right inside, everything is permitted!" Sartre sells tickets to the maze and Camus operates the lightless ferris wheel which never stops yet never progresses. Richardson shills people into the inner darkness where the girlie show bumps and groans in the night, and Conrad mans the turnstile to Jungle Land. Dickens and Hardy, uniformed men to be respected, patrol the midway and enforce the rules. Unlike most amusement parks, however, in the Fowles world illusion becomes reality rather than vice versa. Real tigers stalk the jungles instead of stuffed, prerecorded ones. Fair maidens, damsels in distress, suddenly change into depraved porno movie stars. Unicorns turn into red-hot poker wielding Nazi torturers. Some customers, like Miranda, descend into the cave of horrors never to return. Others, like Nicholas, enter the maze only to emerge shaken and changed. Still others visit the quaint Victorian village area unprepared for the tension lurking beneath its seemingly placid surface. But Fowles's island park is firmly anchored by two solid, deeply-set pilings. These are his central themes: art and life, the aesthetic and the existential. The theme of art is tonal and reveals, often by means of his own voice, the author's personal aesthetic theories. The theme of life is structural, presented in the plots, images, and characterizations of the novels. Thus, from the solid anchoring of his central themes to the philosophic apogee of his Camusian, dark ferris wheel, Fowles creates his novel world. And above the barking Dostoevsky at the main entrance hangs a sign that reads, "Tradition, Art, and the Loneliness of Selfhood." These are the three major concerns and the unifying elements of Fowles's fiction. And therefore, they are also the titles of the three sections of this study of Fowles's mind and art.

Part I, "Tradition," examines the literary foundations upon which Fowles builds his world. Art never exists in isolation or in total originality. Each new art work exists as a part of genre. The work partakes of the past even as it defines the present and prophesies the future. But the genre is organic, always in process. New branches develop but they always grow out of what came before, like a tree with its roots firmly embedded in the humus of the past growing taller and fuller each year. This organicism is Fowles's strength as he moves from the genre of traditional fiction to his own brand of metafiction. Part II, "Art (and Pornography)," explores the theme of art and its relationship to life which appears in each successive novel. Fowles's representation and condemnation of the pornographic impulse in men serves as a contrast to his affirmation of art, especially the art of life. In his novels Fowles defines an aesthetic philosophy. As the novelist's intrusions into *The French Lieutenant's Woman* and the very existence of *The Aristos* testify, Fowles is a writer stalking himself. Or better, he is a novelist writing into a mirror so that each of his works reflects back upon his own mind and vision. Part III, "The Loneliness of Selfhood," defines Fowles's existential theme, his characters' quest for authenticity. This section concentrates upon the images and situations which embody Fowles's existentialism, and upon the endings which dramatize that theme most intensely. Fowles is aware in his fiction of what can be called the existential imperative: modern man's attempt to establish a personal identity in a world hostile to the individual self.

Reflection upon the novel genre and the role of the novelist, the relationship between art and life, the pornographic impulse in human beings, the possibilities (and impossibilities) for existence, and intersubjectivity in the mid-twentieth-century world: These are Fowles's major concerns. As a contemporary writer, John Fowles is an anomaly, almost a literary contradiction. He is both a traditional writer and an innovative metafictionist. He draws upon past literature but changes the direction of the tradition in which he writes. He simultaneously accepts and rejects the literary past, while at the same time he questions contemporary avant-garde attempts to redefine the novel genre. His fiction is a centrifuge in which past and future, time and space, can warp together.


## TRADITION

IN his essay "Notes on an Unfinished Novel," in which he describes the initial conception and the process of writing *The French Lieutenant's Woman*, John Fowles asks himself two questions: "To what extent am I being a coward by writing inside the old tradition? To what extent am I being panicked into avant-gardism?"[1] His very act of posing these two questions in the same paragraph defines his real position and signals his quest for a middle ground between the two extremes. Just as *The French Lieutenant's Woman*, written in an intentionally anachronistic style (Mrs. Poulteney is, for example, an "inhabitant of the Victorian valley of the dolls"), strives to bring together the Victorian past and the mid-twentieth-century present in order to define a moral and existential stance for the future, so also does Fowles in each novel strive to unite the traditional influences which he cannot reject with the new fictional forms of his own conception which he cannot ignore.

The contemporary novelist is like a child who learns and develops by imitating, but who must ulti-

1. *Afterwords: Novelists on Their Novels* (New York, 1969), 165.

mately rebel against the influence of the father in order to define his own selfhood. First following, then—sometimes violently—swerving away from the father's influence, the novelist in his art can display all of the symptoms of an aesthetic Oedipal complex. Iris Murdoch, for example, writes a new theological form of Gothic novel. And Anthony Burgess, while exhibiting many other qualities, is intimately Joycean. The novels of the past do participate in the novels of the present. Always for the serious novelist, however, influence serves as what Georges Poulet calls *"le point de départ"* from which he can move into his own brave new worlds, new situations, and new fictional forms.

Before he began writing novels, John Fowles was Oxford-trained to become a teacher of English literature. He is an extremely well-read novelist. In English literature he seems especially drawn to Shakespeare, and the poets and nonfiction prose writers of the nineteenth century—Tennyson, Matthew Arnold, Darwin, John Stuart Mill—and he frequently alludes to these authors and their works in his fiction. Indeed, *The French Lieutenant's Woman* is a garden of earthly delights for the influence-chasing critic. So many names are dropped, so many quotations are used whose presence must be explained; it is such a scholarly novel, that it seems to be aimed especially at the well-read professor of Victorian literature. Fortunately, however, Fowles never allows *The French Lieutenant's Woman* to be found guilty of these charges. The novel's scholarliness is an essential part of the irony and, quite often, an object of the satire.

The bulk of Fowles's reading, however, has been in the genre in which he writes. At one time or another in his novels he alludes to each of the prominent men and women who preceded him and established the form of British fiction: Jane Austen, Dickens, George Eliot, Conrad, and, of course, Hardy. But he does not restrict himself to British fiction. He seems particularly drawn to the major Continental philosopher-novelists: Dostoevsky, Camus, Sartre.

For a novelist as knowledgeable as Fowles in the past of his genre and in the philosophical thought of his time, the definition of influences is especially important. Even more important is the definition of the complex manner in which Fowles uses and reacts to the literary and philosophical influences upon his fiction. Invariably, like the child opposing the father, he rebels against an influence, reshapes it, or redefines it in a modern context. At times, as in *The French Lieutenant's Woman*, he actually parodies and satirizes his source material. Also, since Fowles is an overtly philosophical novelist, a correspondence between his philosophical ideas (the abstract themes of his novels, which stem from philosophical influences) and his novelistic style (the characterizations, images, and situations that stem from literary influences) exists and can be defined. Therefore, the influences upon Fowles's thought are equal in importance to the literary influences upon his novels, and *The Aristos* provides a glass through which one can see darkly into the landscape of the author's mind.

Ostensibly, the major philosophical influence upon *The Aristos* was the Greek scientist, Heraclitus, from whom Fowles got the title for his book. For Heraclitus the "aristos" was "the good man" who displayed "independence of judgment" and who pursued "inner wisdom and inner knowledge" (216). But the concepts of Heraclitus serve only as classical metaphors representing the individuality and self-awareness that Fowles hopes his own philosophical treatise will foster. The framework of Fowles's thought in *The Aristos* and in the novels, is, as Fowles readily states, existentialist:

> Existentialism is conspicuously unsuited to political or social subversion, since it is incapable of organized dogmatic resistance or formulations of resistance. It is capable only of one man's resistance; one personal expression of view; such as this book. (123)

Thus, Fowles's philosophy is existentialist but his assertion of that fact does not demand immediate obeisance to Sartre and Camus and Kierkegaard. As Fowles himself writes in *The Aristos*, "The first existentialist was Socrates, not Kierkegaard" (122). Heraclitus also was an existentialist, as was Pascal whose *Pensées* gave Fowles not only the rhetorical format for *The Aristos* (a collection of numbered aphoristic notations) but also one of the book's basic metaphors (the bet situation).

What each of these philosophers have in common with Sartre and Camus and what endears them all to Fowles is the affirmation, in earlier times and in different places, of the dominant ideals of existentialism. Ultimately, Fowles concerns himself with the problems of self-definition, of individuality, of freedom, of choice, and of revolt. For Fowles, existentialism "tries to re-establish in the individual a sense of his own uniqueness" (122). A man coming alive to himself in an absurd world of both literal and metaphorical death (such as the death of selfhood or the death of love) is Fowles's, and Heraclitus's, and Camus's, concept of an "aristos" or "good man."

Perhaps because Fowles is both a philosopher–novelist and an optimist, his closest allegiance among contemporary thinkers is to Albert Camus. Both in their writings openly perceive the absurd and with

Sisyphean dedication rebel against it; for Fowles, "as man sees through one reason for living, another wells from the mysterious spring. It must be so because he continues to exist. This inexplicable buoyancy irritates him. He exists, but he is abused" (16). Fowles's modern man is always "miserably *en passage*" (15) as is Camus's Sisyphus perpetually struggling with his rock. As Sisyphus, Camus, and Fowles all realize, only action has value and results are not necessary, or even desirable, because the accomplishment of a result can put a halt to action. "We build towards nothing; we build" (19), writes Fowles with Camusian terseness. This emphasis upon process rather than result perhaps best explains the persistent open-endedness of Fowles's novels.

In *The Myth of Sisyphus*, while discussing "absurd freedom," Camus writes:

> Knowing whether or not one can live *without appeal* is all that interests me . . . let's avoid romanticism and just ask ourselves what such an attitude may mean to a man with his mind made up to take up his bet. . . . Being aware of one's life, one's revolt, one's freedom, and to the maximum, is living, and to the maximum . . . the point is to live.[2]

In *The Aristos*, Fowles closely echoes Camus even in the allusion to the Pascalian bet:

> The idea of an afterlife has persistently haunted man. . . . This myth was a compensatory fantasy, a psychological safety-valve for the frustrations of existential reality. . . . We *must* bet on the other horse: we have one life. . . . What matters is not our personal damnation or salvation in the world to come, but that of our fellow men in the world that is. (30–31)

2. *The Myth of Sisyphus and Other Essays* (New York, 1955), 44–48.

For both Fowles and Camus existence is all, and they write for those who would squander existence on unpromising, long-shot bets. Fowles's basic interest, like Camus's, is in a real personal salvation on earth rather than in a romantic and unreal dependence upon the promise, made by an absent God, of an afterlife. Each of Fowles's novels, therefore, concerns a central character who must come alive to that basic Camusian premise, "The point is to live."

But who influenced Camus? Who planted the seeds of existential thought which yielded first *The Myth of Sisyphus* and then later, *The Aristos*? Just prior to his sudden death, Camus wrote:

> As I lived through the cruel drama of my epoch I began to love in Dostoevsky one who has lived and expressed most profoundly our historical destiny. For me, Dostoevsky is first of all a writer who, long before Nietzsche, knew how to discern modern nihilism, to define it and predict its monstrous consequences and to try to indicate the road to salvation.[3]

Just as numerous references to and echoes of Dostoevsky appear in *The Myth of Sisyphus*, so also do Dostoevskian echoes reverberate throughout *The Aristos*, especially echoes of "The Legend of the Grand Inquisitor" from *The Brothers Karamazov*. Though Fowles never mentions Dostoevsky in *The Aristos* as he does Heraclitus, Pascal, Kierkegaard, Camus, and Sartre, the shadow of the Grand Inquisitor is there, punctuating and underlining the book's ideas.

Dostoevsky in his legend examines, through the Inquisitor's totalitarian rationalism, the questions of the existence of God and the nature of human happi-

3. "The Other Russia," *New York Herald Tribune*, 19 December 1957.

ness. The Grand Inquisitor leads an earthly church which strives for men to "lay their freedom at our feet, and say to us, 'Make us your slaves, but feed us.' " This church is concerned only with man's earthly, bodily "happiness," the happiness of a full belly and an untroubled mind—the happiness of a contented animal. The Inquisitor asks Christ, "Man was created a rebel; and how can rebels be happy?" and he tells Christ how the church has finally "vanquished freedom . . . to make men happy." He describes the church's plans to take away man's "fearful burden of free choice" and turn mankind into "a flock of sheep, grateful and obedient," creating a life with no mystery in which the church's leaders will "have an answer for all."[4] This symbolic legend of the Spanish Inquisition incorporates the either–or alternatives that are open to twentieth-century man. Shall I be free and authentic and miserable, in my selfhood facing all the anxieties of existential life? Or shall I be happy and give up my freedom and identity to a society that will impose an external essence upon my existence?

Early in *The Aristos* Fowles, echoing Dostoevsky's Inquisitor, examines from a rationalist position the reasons for the disappearance of God and the concepts of freedom of belief and mystery:

> A god who revealed his will, who "heard" us . . . such a god would destroy all our hazard, all our purpose and all our happiness. . . .
> What we call suffering, death, disaster, misfortune, tragedy, we should call the price of freedom. The only alternative to this suffering freedom is an unsuffering unfreedom. (18–19)

Like Dostoevsky in *The Brothers Karamazov*, Fowles in *The Aristos* is primarily concerned with both the

4. Modern Library Edition (New York, 1950), 293–312.

nature of God and the nature of man. He realizes, as
did Dostoevsky, that if God is to continue to exist in
any form and if man is to maintain any freedom, God
must remain unseen and mysterious. "We go on living," Fowles writes, "because we do not know why
we are here to live. Unknowing, or hazard, is as vital
to man as water" (27). He directly echoes Dostoevsky's
Inquisitor by defining and discussing the value of
mystery:

> Mystery, or unknowing, is energy. As soon as a mys-
> tery is explained, it ceases to be a source of energy. If we
> question deep enough there comes a point where an-
> swers, if answers could be given, would kill. . . . In fact,
> since "God" is unknowable, we cannot dam the spring
> of basic existential mystery. "God" is the energy of all
> questions and questing; and so the ultimate source of
> all action and volition. (28)

Both Fowles and Dostoevsky express the idea that if
freedom is to continue to exist in the world, God as a
seeable, knowable, definable entity must remain absent from the world. God's existence must remain only
metaphorical, like the pillar of fire that burns in the
mind of the madman, Henrik Nygaard, in the Seidevarre section of *The Magus*.

Fowles's *Aristos*, as did Dostoevsky's legend,
also focuses upon the nature of organized religion.
For Fowles, the "Christian churches . . . have frequently made their own self-continuance their chief
pre-occupation . . . they have set themselves up as
refuges and too often taken good care that outside
their doors refuge shall be needed" (105–6). Further-
more, churches have surrounded the fundamental mystery of the existence and nature of God with a "fair-
ground of pseudo-mysteries" unrelated to any truth
but *"only to the truth that mystery has power"* (108).

**11**

Dostoevsky's Inquisitor burns with a mad, irreligious dream of the priests gaining total control over the masses who will give up their freedom in exchange for bread. Fowles uses a somewhat different image, yet the meaning is the same: "The Many are like an audience under the spell of a conjuror, seemingly unable to do anything but serve as material for the conjuror's tricks" (213). The irony of the image is that the audience, if it wishes, can always walk out of the theater; the worshipper can arise and leave the church, turn his back on the conjurors of organized religion; and Christ, after offering the kiss of peace to the Grand Inquisitor, can silently walk from the prison, unmiraculous; leaving undisturbed man's freedom to believe. Like the Christ-figure in Dostoevsky's legend, the conjuror–god Conchis of *The Magus* must silently abscond from the world that he has created if human freedom is ever to exist in that world.

But Fowles is neither a philosopher nor a theologian; he is a novelist. *The Aristos* is significant because it reveals Fowles's attitudes toward the modern world. If we know how Fowles thinks, then we are better equipped to understand the metaphors of his mind, his novels. As Albert Camus wrote, "A novel is never anything but a philosophy expressed in images. And in a good novel the philosophy has disappeared into the images."[5] Fowles's novels profit from his philosophical reading, but they are influenced even more by his extensive knowledge of the past of the novel genre.

In each of his novels, Fowles establishes a pattern of recurring allusion to one or more prior works of literature. He is often quite explicit in his use of literary analogies, and these analogies are usually fully developed rather than suggestive. While he draws

5. *Lyrical and Critical Essays* (New York, 1968), 199.

parallels between the characters and the situations of his present novel and those of a work of the past, he also often evokes the imagery and the moral themes of the previous work which he has chosen as his point of analogical focus. For example, the social derangement of Clegg in *The Collector* is connected by repeated analogical reference to Caliban of Shakespeare's *The Tempest*. Both Rosemary Laughlin and Jeff Rackham have explicated Fowles's use of Shakespeare's play, the most obvious influence upon *The Collector*.[6] But *The Tempest* is but one, however, and not even the most important, of many sources for *The Collector*'s situations and characterizations.

In *The Collector* Fowles juggles his literary source material with the facility of a performer born and raised on a circus midway. As his hand touches upon one influence, the others remain tangibly present though temporarily suspended in mid-air. As one influence moves away, another descends to replace it in his hand. And thus the influences upon his novel revolve faster and faster by the juggler's art until they no longer are separate entities but rather become a pattern in motion, a whole composed of moving complementary parts, a new reality created by the combination and transformation of a number of old realities. In *The Collector*, Fowles alludes to situations and images from Conrad's *Lord Jim*, Dostoevsky's *Crime and Punishment*, Dickens's *Great Expectations*, and Jane Austen's *Emma*, as well as Shakespeare's *The Tempest*.

The central image of *The Collector*, the butterfly, mirrors Stein's symbolic butterflies, which appear at the very center of *Lord Jim*. In Conrad's novel, both Stein and Marlow are collectors. Stein collects, pins,

6. *Critique*, 13, 3, pp. 74. 83, and pp. 92–93.

and classifies his butterflies while Marlow collects all the available information about Jim and then tries to capture Jim's existence, to classify him as either a coward or a romantic hero or as "one of us." Butterflies and human beings—Clegg collects and classifies both.

A number of Clegg's dreams are described in *The Collector* and each one invites comparison with the frenzied dreams of Raskolnikov in *Crime and Punishment*. Clegg describes one dream in which he tries to kill Miranda: "I hit and hit and she laughed and then I jumped on her and smothered her and she lay still, and then when I took the cushion away she was lying there laughing" (74). This dream directly echoes Raskolnikov's third dream in which he, for the first time, becomes the brutal protagonist in one of his own dreams as he attempts to beat to death the old pawnbroker who woodenly sits in her corner and laughs at him.

At another point in *The Collector*, Clegg's sense of the loss of his mother, which was heightened by his dislike for her replacement, Aunt Annie, is compared by Miranda to Pip's situation in Dickens's *Great Expectations*. In a direct Dickensian allusion, Miranda equates Clegg and his Aunt Annie to "Mrs. Joe and Pip" (170). Echoing Pip's great expectations, Clegg breaks from the influence of the mother surrogate and aspires to the love of a beautiful woman of a higher class who can never love him. Miranda is Clegg's unreachable Estella.

One of the most significant influences upon *The Collector*, an influence that defines the characterization of Miranda, is Jane Austen's *Emma*. "I *am* Emma Woodhouse," Miranda writes in her diary, "I know she does wrong things . . . yet all the time one knows she's basically intelligent, alive. . . . Her faults are my faults: her virtues I must *make* my virtues" (146–47). Miranda recognizes in herself and in Jane Austen's fictional character the same immaturity, the same lack of experience in the perception of reality; but she also senses the same potential for growth and development into real humanity. *Emma* becomes Miranda's metaphor for her own situation: the "business of being between inexperienced girl and experienced woman and the awful problem of *the* man. Caliban is Mr. Elton. Piers is Frank Churchill. But is G. P. Mr. Knightley?" (202). Unfortunately, Miranda's metaphor breaks down because the world of *The Collector* is not a comic world like Jane Austen's and Miranda cannot easily solve her problem as Emma could. Miranda cannot "arrange a marriage" for Clegg, some "little Harriet Smith, with whom he could be mousy and sane and happy" (196). Ultimately, the world of *The Collector* swerves away from the sanity and order of Jane Austen's comic world, and Miranda's metaphor becomes a wistful illusion as the novel descends into the insane, chaotic world of tragedy.

Fowles makes no direct allusion however, to the one novel that exercises the strongest influence upon the plot, narrative technique, and characterization of *The Collector*. But that novel's influence—it began the psychological tradition within the English novel— broods over all of the tragic action of *The Collector*. In many ways, *The Collector* is a twentieth-century version of Samuel Richardson's *Clarissa*.

In narrative technique, *The Collector* is an epistolary novel. Miranda's diary is a collection of letters written "to the moment" as are Clarissa Harlowe's. "I can't write in a vacuum like this. To no one," Miranda writes. She then begins her next descriptive passage as a letter: "Dear Minny. I have been here over a week now and I miss you very much." (117). Fowles fully exploits the potential for relativistic narrative of the epistolary form, as did Richardson. By means of juxtaposed first-person narratives that focus on the same events, both Richardson and Fowles create a psychological tension between the opposing male and female views. The reader thus can gauge the separation of sensibility and pinpoint the breakdown in communication that in both *The Collector* and *Clarissa* ultimately cause the tragic denouement. *The Collector*, with its concentration upon the inner lives and motivations of its characters as expressed in their own words, stands solidly in the epistolary-psychological tradition that Richardson began.

The plots of both *Clarissa* and *The Collector* are also strikingly similar. In Richardson's novel, Lovelace lures Clarissa away from her family and into the depths of London where he, with the help of a crew of obligingly sadistic whores, effectively holds her prisoner in a brothel. Fowles's Miranda is torn away from her normal life and held captive in an underground world cut off from all humanity. Both the eighteenth-century heroine and her twentieth-century counterpart make numerous escape attempts and write pleas for help in letters which are never mailed. Finally, both heroines are drugged and raped by their male captors who, realizing that neither heroine will ever consent to a natural sexual relationship, choose to destroy their humanity and possess them by degrading them. Fowles, however, adds a particularly modern nuance to his rape scene. Like Lovelace, Clegg drugs his victim, but because he is impotent, he "rapes" her with his camera. Whereas Lovelace senses his own impotence in his inability to penetrate into Clarissa's selfhood only after he has committed the unnatural act. Clegg's acknowledged impotence heightens the unnaturalness of his relationship with Miranda. In the end both heroines die, alone in small, closed rooms; their humanity violated, their lives turned into nightmares.

Both Clegg and Lovelace are also similar types of impresarios; both fantasize constantly and both are obsessed with the desire to turn fantasy life into real life. They desire to possess the ethereal heroines of the pornographic movies that flicker in their perverse imagination. Even the images of sadism-masochism are comparable. Where Richardson uses the recurring image of the male hunter trapping his defenseless female prey, Fowles uses the image of the collector capturing the defenseless butterfly and destroying its beauty and life. *Clarissa* can, however, influence *The Collector* only to a certain point, a point where the past must end and the present must assert its own reality. Richardson wrote *Clarissa* for a still Christian age that believed in religion, justice among men, and an afterlife. If a man scoffed at religion and violated human rights, honorable men usually sent him to the afterlife before his time. Just as Lovelace lived by his phallic sword, he died by the honorable sword of justice. But Fowles is writing for a much less ordered world, for an age in which evil can and frequently does triumph over justice. And Clegg, not even slightly touched by the kind of remorse that Lovelace felt, blithely prepares the underground room for its next guest.

*The Magus* also reflects the eclectic influence of earlier novel writers. Dickens and Dostoevsky exercise major influence, but Conrad exerts the heaviest pressure upon the events and images of Fowles's second novel. Dickens and Dostoevsky are first mentioned in a speech by Conchis who declares that the "novel is dead" and then goes on to tell Nicholas how one day he "burnt every novel. . . . Dickens. Cervantes. Dostoevsky. Flaubert. All the great and all the small. . . . Words are for truth. For facts. Not fiction" (92). Ironically, Nicholas is led into a Dostoevskian world in which Conchis carries the weight of the novelist's responsibility as either omniscient narrator (relating the stories of the past) or as dramatist (choreographing the scenes of the masque). Twice Nicholas uses the same phrase, from Dostoevsky's *The Brothers Karamazov*, to describe Conchis's fictional world: "Nothing is true, everything is permitted" (389, 477). Conchis reconstructs the past, complete, with seventeenth-century murderers, Victorian virgins, and Nazi sadists, brings the myths of Isis and Anubis–Cerberus to life, and manipulates the lives and loves of people in the present as though they were so many puppets on a string. In this way, he becomes a personification of the God who plagues Ivan Karamazov's mind, a God who has created and maintained a world that, as Nicholas Urfe sees it, has "no limits in this masque, no normal social laws or conventions" (196).

Echoes of Ivan's "Legend of the Grand Inquisitor" also reverberate throughout *The Magus*. Conchis's realization, as he stands alone in the square with an empty machine gun and the responsibility for killing the *Eleutheria* man, the Greek freedom fighter, is the embodiment of the meaning of Ivan's "poem in prose":

> The word was in his eyes, in his being, totally in his being. What did Christ say on the cross? Why hast thou forsaken me? What this man said was something far less sympathetic, far less pitiful, even far less human, but far profounder. He spoke out of a world the very

opposite of mine. In mine life had no price. It was so valuable that it was literally priceless. In his, only one thing had that quality of pricelessness. It was *eleutheria*: freedom. . . . I saw that I was the only person left in that square who had the freedom left to choose, and that the annunciation and defense of that freedom was more important than common sense, self-preservation, yes, than my own life. (394–95)

The object of Conchis's godgame is self-realization in the novice, the victim, the audience of one, or whatever role Nicholas is playing at the time. And the godgame is always mysterious because, as Conchis says, "An answer is always a death" (575). This one fact, concerning both God and man, is the truth that burns in the heart of the old man in Ivan's legend.

While Dostoevskian implications help define the nature of the world and the theme of freedom in *The Magus*, Fowles's narrative structure and the mythic implications present in the confrontation between Conchis and Nicholas are reminiscent of two of the major concerns of Joseph Conrad's novels. Conchis, as he takes his seat on the darkened verandah at Bourani and, with Nicholas for an audience, reaches back into his own past, is much like Marlow sitting on similar verandahs or on the decks of anchored ships spinning similar webs of meaning out into the darkness. When Conchis pauses in the midst of his story—"Let us have some brandy,"—he directly echoes Marlow's more frequent "Pass the bottle" in "Youth." And the atmosphere of Conchis's storytelling seances—"1914 and 1953 were eons apart; 1914 was on a planet circling one of the furthest faintest stars. The vast stretch, the pace of time" (115)—is the same atmosphere that Conrad's narrator creates for his listeners in *Heart of Darkness*:

The Thames stretched before us like the beginning of an interminable waterway . . . the sea and sky were welded together without a joint . . . the sky, without a speck, was a benign immensity of unstained light . . . a waterway leading to the uttermost ends of the earth.[7]

In the midst of one of his reveries of the past, as he talks of the wealth of his own mentor, De Deukans, Conchis makes direct reference to a central plot source of *The Magus*. He tells Nicholas:

"The great bulk of his money was in various enterprises in the Congo. Givray-le-Duc, like the Parthenon, was built on a heart of darkness."
"Is Bourani built on it?"
"Would you leave at once if I said it was?"
"No."
"Then you have no right to ask." (183)

Nicholas Urfe's journey into the dark existential masque of Bourani is a journey into the heart of darkness, into the depths of self-consciousness. Nicholas's guide on this night journey is kin to Marlow's guide; Conchis is a mid-twentieth-century Kurtz who holds the same fascination of abomination for Nicholas that Conrad's representative of the reality of the human condition held for Marlow.

The shadow of Dickens is also quite conspicuous in *The Magus*. Individual scenes and descriptions recall Dickensian analogs. For example, at one point Fowles ironically employs a famous Dickensian phrase to characterize the phoniness of Nicholas in his relationship with Alison: "I pressed her shoulders as if, really, it was a far, far better thing that I did then than woman could easily imagine" (238). The most obvious Dickensian allusion appears in a brief interlude near

7. Norton Critical Edition (New York, 1963), 3–4.

the end of *The Magus*. Nicholas, "full of kindness to dumb animals," takes up with a dirty, homely, and homeless waif named Jojo. She is "someone worthy of a modern Mayhew . . . douce as rain—London rain, because she was seldom very clean—and utterly without ambition or meanness . . . grateful for the smallest bone, like an old mongrel" (583–84). Jojo is a twentieth-century reincarnation of "poor Jo," the homeless crossing sweep, for whom Dickens probably found inspiration in the pages of Mayhew and fleshed out in his own *Bleak House*.

The influence of the Marquis de Sade and Thomas Carlyle, both of whom combine philosophical writing with fictional technique, also casts a significant shadow over the events and characterizations of *The Magus*. Fowles's epigraphs for each of the three sections of *The Magus* are from De Sade's *Les Infortunes de la Vertu*. The epigraph that opens Part One—"*Un débauché de profession est rarement un homme pitoyable*"—prefigures the characterization of Nicholas Urfe in this short, London-based introductory section. He is a cynical, professional rake and, like De Sade's libertines, he is unable to love Alison, unable to feel the hurt that he is causing her. The epigraph for the second section of the novel is a description of torturers mangling the loins of a miserable, helpless victim. This description prefigures Conchis's story of the violent deaths of the Greek freedom fighters at the hands of the sadistic Nazis, and it stands at the beginning of a section in which successive descriptions of atrocity and violence culminate with Nicholas standing alone in a Sade-like situation. He must choose between tearing the helpless female flesh with the vicious cat (which would culminate Conchis's history of twentieth-century violence in a temporally immediate act) or affirming his own and his prospective victim's humanity by denying the necessity of subhuman violence.

The third De Sade epigraph is a definition of the purpose of philosophy. Philosophy should, De Sade wrote, illuminate the relationship between man and that providence which rules the world so haphazardly. It should trace a "plan of conduct" by which man could interpret the demands made upon him by his contemporary world. Fittingly, then, in Part Three of *The Magus* Fowles's central character, Nicholas, tries to understand the meaning of his experiences in the first two parts of the novel and finally apply this newfound, "philosophical" knowledge to his own personal existence.

The Carlylean influence, like the De Sade influence, illuminates both the characterization of Nicholas and the specific events in his life. Throughout the early part of *The Magus*, Nicholas performs a highly literary impersonation. He does a Teufelsdröckhian impression of Lord Byron until finally heeding Carlyle's warning from *Sartor Resartus* to "Close thy Byron." When Nicholas first imagines going to Greece he can only visualize "Byron's death at Missolonghi" (36); then he takes a job at the Lord Byron School. Alone in an unimaginative, asexual world, Nicholas immerses himself in a Carlylean form of Byronism. In his farcical attempted suicide, Nicholas, like Teufelsdröckh, descends into "The Everlasting No." "The whole world had finally declared itself against me," Nicholas says, and he feels "filled with nothingness; with something more than the old physical and social loneliness" (54). Alone and abandoned, he walks "in hell" (54) as Teufelsdröckh did in the "*Rue Saint-Thomas de Enfer.*"

Thus, by entering "The Everlasting No," Nicholas begins his journey to selfhood.

Whereas ideas, characters, and events in *The Magus* reflect the material of past literature and align that material with the context of the twentieth-century world, in *The French Lieutenant's Woman* plot and characterization, image and idea, consciously imitate specific Victorian sources for two antagonistic reasons. First, the plot and characterizations of *The French Lieutenant's Woman* emanate from two basic Victorian fictional sources, Thomas Hardy's *A Pair of Blue Eyes* and Dickens's *Pickwick Papers,* because of what seems initially to be Fowles's whole intention for his novel: to recreate the ambience of both the world and the literary style of the novel genre's period of greatest accomplishment, the Victorian Age. But secondly, Fowles turns upon his own sources, parodies them, and finally shows how the twentieth-century artist must rebel against the restrictions upon narrative technique, characterization, and content that were established by the Victorian novel and have survived to plague the twentieth-century novelist.

I have elsewhere, in collaboration with A. A. DeVitis, examined in detail Fowles's use of Hardy's *A Pair of Blue Eyes* as a source for *The French Lieutenant's Woman.*[8] However, Fowles's use of *The Pickwick Papers* as a source and influence demonstrates equally well his rebellion against the Victorian novel. Like Dickens, Fowles creates broadly comic characters and starkly realized grotesques to populate the subplots and backgrounds of his novel. By means of the realistic modernization and, hence, de-sentimentalizing of some of Dickens's best-known character types,

8. *Contemporary Literature*, 15, i (Winter 1974).

Fowles vividly demonstrates the difference between Victorian fiction and the mid-twentieth-century novel.

The most obviously Dickensian character is Sam Farrow, Charles Smithson's manservant, who is ostensibly a later nineteenth-century version of Pickwick's lively companion, Sam Weller. However, the reader is shocked by this new Sam's deviation from the expected Pickwickian norm. As the narrator explains, this new Sam is indeed different:

> To us any Cockney servant called Sam evokes immediately the immortal Weller; and it was certainly from that background that this Sam had emerged. But thirty years had passed since *Pickwick Papers* first coruscated into the world. . . . The difference between Sam Weller and Sam Farrow (that is, between 1836 and 1867) was this: the first was happy with his role, the second suffered it. (39–40)

Where simple moral decisions were resolved for the best immediately and instinctively by Dickens's Sam Weller, Sam Farrow's moral instincts are effectively anesthetized in a very twentieth-century manner. Fowles's Sam is, after all, the precursor of the twentieth-century advertising man, Madison Avenue style. Evolution, so the stereotype proclaims, has favored the modern businessman with a highly developed sense of barracuda opportunism while dooming to extinction any moral inclinations he might have had. This is the way Darwinian natural selection operates—choosing, eliminating, and refining—from Sam Weller to Sam Farrow to the man in the grey flannel suit, and moral instinct becomes unfit for survival.

Another starkly realized Dickensian character in *The French Lieutenant's Woman* is the grotesque Mrs. Poulteney, who mimics the styles and attitudes of characters like the evil dwarf Quilp in *The Old Curi-*

*osity Shop* or Madame LaFarge in *A Tale of Two Cities* or Miss Wade in *Little Dorrit*, characters whose own lives are so warped that their only pleasure comes from the persecution of other human beings. Mrs. Poulteney, for example, delights in having Sarah Woodruff, whose virginity has been questioned because of her supposed elopement with the French Lieutenant, read aloud the 119th Psalm, "Blessed are the undefiled!"

Thus, *The French Lieutenant's Woman* is initially aligned with the eminent Victorian tradition of Dickens and Hardy, but soon it rebels against that tradition. *The French Lieutenant's Woman* consciously recreates the Dickens world (and the Hardy world simultaneously). But it also brings those worlds up to date and portrays them with a reality that Dickens and Hardy, because of the Victorian restrictions upon the novel genre, could not present.

Though Dickens and Hardy exert the most obvious influences upon *The French Lieutenant's Woman*, Fowles's writing reflects others. In fact, perhaps *The French Lieutenant's Woman* is really what Northrop Frye would call an "anatomy" rather than a novel. Like Burton's *Anatomy of Melancholy* or Carlyle's *Sartor Resartus*, it is a collection of many different elements besides the fictional plot. For example, the epigraphs that open each chapter attest to the variety of the materials upon which Fowles has drawn in his conception of theme and action in his novel.

These epigraphs can be analyzed in terms of three major categories. First, the novel opens with a quotation from Karl Marx—"*Every emancipation is a restoration of the human world and of human relationships to man himself*"—which is a general definition of humanness: When a man is most free, he is most human. At intervals thereafter, five more Marxian epigraphs appear. Each is either a portrait of the dehumanized condition of the laboring classes or a basic definition of the nature of the human condition. The second category is comprised of scientific testimony to the nature of life in this world. The writings of Charles Darwin dominate this set of epigraphs, but he is supported by quotations from both physical scientists, such as Martin Gardner, and social scientists, such as E. Royston Pike and G. M. Young. These scientific epigraphs help to define both Charles Smithson's situation in Victorian England, that of an aristocrat who has been naturally selected for extinction by a rising middle class more fit to survive, and the meaning of one of the main imagistic motifs of the novel, the motif of fossils.

The third category, comprising the largest number of epigraphs, is Victorian poetry. Four major Victorian poets, Tennyson, Clough, Arnold, and Hardy, contribute almost fifty quotations. The Hardy excerpts help to set the scene (as do a number of quotations about Lyme from Jane Austen's *Persuasion*) especially by means of repeated allusion to a poem entitled "At a Seaside Town in 1869." The quotations from Clough concentrate upon two conflicting ideas: duty, which for Clough means conformity to social demands in all their meaninglessness; and introspective self-analysis as stimulated by love. In Charles Smithson these two modes of action clash stridently. Tennyson is quoted more often than any of the other poets and these epigraphs are drawn exclusively from *Maud* and *In Memoriam*. *Maud* examines the changes that occur in the personality of a man who becomes involved in a love relationship that rubs against the grain of Victorian propriety. Though Tennyson's melancholy hero is a poor man in love with a rich girl and Fowles's is a nobleman in love with a governess, both poem and novel delve into similar existential tensions. And Charles Smithson might well declare, as the hero of *Maud* does, "And ah for a man to arise in me, / That the man I am may cease to be!" (266). *In Memoriam* captures, perhaps better than any other Victorian poem, the doubts and the fears of that age, and its recurring presence contributes greatly to the reader's sense of Victorian insecurity and fear of change. But of the four poets, Arnold seems to hold the most meaning for Fowles's novel.

Arnold's poetry speaks of sadness and isolation: the isolation of a man aware that he must define his own identity and the sadness of a man who realizes that he must make painful decisions in accordance with that defined identity. In *The French Lieutenant's Woman* Fowles employs epigraphs from four Arnold poems, all of which demonstrate the Arnoldian feeling of the loneliness of selfhood. The two quotations from "A Farewell" describe the feverish tension that love places upon the human heart and the two quotations from "Parting" describe the pain present in willed separation from a lover. Charles Smithson is a prisoner of the feverish tension of his love for Sarah throughout the novel, and in the end he chooses (perhaps, depending on the ending that the reader chooses) the pain of separation as the speaker in "Parting" does. The quotation from "Self-Dependence" describes a man weary from the effort of trying to define himself, and the quotation from "The Scholar–Gipsy" advises solitude as the situation necessary for self-definition. By the end of *The French Lieutenant's Woman*, Charles, already weary from the ordeal of the quest for selfhood, takes Arnold's advice and (again, according to one's choice of ending) chooses the solitude necessary for the continuation of the quest.

But Arnold's influence is not restricted to representation only in the epigraphs of this novel as Tennyson and Clough are. Quite early in the novel Charles Smithson is described as thinking "like Matthew Arnold" (125) and much later the narrator quotes in its entirety "perhaps the noblest short poem of the whole Victorian era," Arnold's "To Marguerite" (334–35). This poem's haunting images of separation and isolation and "mortal millions" living alone defines, better than any of the epigraphs, the basic situation that the central characters of *The French Lieutenant's Woman* —Ernestina, Sarah, and especially Charles—must accept. Like the persona of Arnold's "Stanzas From the Grand Chartreuse," Charles, quite early in the novel, feels "himself in suspension between the two worlds, the warm, neat civilization behind his back, the cool, dark mystery outside" (123). Ernestina represents the "dead" past and Sarah represents the future that is "impossible to be born." Fowles's novel itself also hangs in this same suspension: between the tradition of Victorian fiction, with its attendant restrictions, and the experimental, intensely self-conscious novel of the mid-twentieth-century.

Thus, Fowles uses Marx and Darwin to give definition to the situation of man in the Victorian world and he employs the many epigraphs from Victorian poetry to illuminate his characterizations and plot situations. The illusion of reading a Victorian novel is heightened by the presence of these epigraphs. Fowles's imitation of Victorian style blends with the original Victorian writing in the epigraphs, and the imitation seems more authentic. Though the foundation of

Fowles's fiction is in the novelists (and the poets and philosophers) of the past, however, his major concern is for the art of the future and the relation of art, in particular his own fiction, to the lives of men.

John Fowles is a "novelist at the crossroads"[9] in his combination of the tradition of his genre with the experimental qualities of contemporary fiction. In *The Collector* he is just approaching the crossroads, his feet still firmly set in the epistolary-psychological tradition of Samuel Richardson. But in *The Magus* and *The French Lieutenant's Woman*, while still able to look back down the traditional road, he strikes off in new experimental directions, moving toward existential metafiction.

## ART (AND PORNOGRAPHY)

IN *The Magus*, as Nicholas Urfe sees the curtain of night fall on Scene One of Conchis's masque— a dramatization of the mythic relationship of Apollo, Artemis–Diana, and man—his mind conjures "vague memories of Oscar Wilde" (179). The masque's analogy between reality and mythic scene and the memories of Wilde, the theorist of the relationship of life to art, warn of the tensions that will soon exert pressure on Nicholas's life. The dramatist–god Conchis– Apollo will control the pursuit, capture and torment of Nick, the satyr–man, by Lily, the huntress Artemis– Diana. Nicholas's thoughts of Wilde define Fowles's dramatic intention. In *The Magus*, life learns to imitate art. Each scene in Conchis's masque functions as an

9. David Lodge, *The Novelist at the Crossroads* (Ithaca, N.Y., 1971).

analogue for imitation in Nicholas's own action later in the novel. The masque's "prehauntings" (179) all later come to life, and are adapted into the modern dress of Nicholas's own experience.

This relationship between art and life is a recurring theme throughout the fiction of John Fowles. Each of Fowles's central characters—Miranda, Nicholas Urfe, Charles Smithson—exists *en passage*. All are trying to give form to the chaos of existence. In a sense, each of these characters is an artist trying to create a living work of art, trying to compose his or her own life.

In *The Collector* the life–art theme is overt, imbedded in Fowles's characterization. Miranda is an embryonic artist, an emerging butterfly, while Clegg is anti-artistic and subconsciously intent upon perverting the art and beauty of life. In *The Magus*, descriptive references to visual and literary art repeatedly define the landscape, the characterizations, and the events of the novel. The artistic dramatization of life, Conchis's elaborate masque, lures Nicholas into participation and awakens him to his potentiality for creating his own existence. And, in *The French Lieutenant's Woman*, the abstract theme of art unfolds simultaneously with the existential theme of the quest for selfhood. While *The French Lieutenant's Woman* certainly concerns the tensions of a love triangle and certainly dramatizes the attempts of the central characters to find selfhood in a world that represses individuality, the plot and the characters also comprise a metaphor for Fowles's aesthetic theme. It is a novel about the past and the future of the novel genre. It deals with Oscar Wilde's central concern in *The Critic as Artist*: "the relations which exist between Art and Life." In each novel Fowles presents characters who try to create, as artists do, new existences out of the chaos of their lives.

Through characterization, metaphor, and, in *The French Lieutenant's Woman*, through overt authorial comment, Fowles develops his life–art theme. For Fowles's characters art becomes the primal stimulus to self-definition, moral action, and finally existential life. Repeatedly, Fowles's central characters—Miranda, Nicholas, Charles—opt for moral decadence. Nicholas tries throughout *The Magus* to edge his personal experience "out of the moral world into the aesthetic, where it was easier to live with" (363), but this sort of easy self-indulgence has no place in the Fowles world. Life must learn to imitate great art's powers for truth-telling and beauty-creating.

The thematic representation of the life–art relationship begins in Fowles's first novel, *The Collector*. Early on in her captivity Miranda asks Clegg,

> "Do you know anything about art?" . . .
> Nothing you'd call knowledge.
> "I knew you didn't. You wouldn't imprison an innocent person if you did."
> I don't see the connection. . . . I'm an entomologist. I collect butterflies.
> "Of course. . . . Now you've collected me." (41)

In this brief dialogue Miranda implies that art offers to all men an emotional, intuitive knowledge of man's moral responsibilities to his fellow man. Art represents justice for the innocent and the recognition of every man's right to be free. Unfortunately, the only kind of knowledge that Clegg respects is scientific, objective knowledge; knowledge that has been deadened by its certainty, which has but one static meaning. Fowles defines the conflict between art and science in *The Aristos* when he writes that "the scientist dehumanizes, someone must humanize. . . . Art . . . is the expression of truths too complex for science to express" (151), and he dramatizes this conflict in the intellectual impasse that develops between Miranda and Clegg.

Miranda knows, because she has learned the idea from her mentor George Paston, that great art is the expression of the very essence of life, a window to the center of the self. For G. P., "living art" must be a "limb of your body." He, almost pendantically (and there is great irony in this because he is analyzing what he himself has declared to be unanalyzable), lectures to Miranda that

> it's what you say that counts. It's what distinguishes all great art from the other kind. The technically accomplished buggers are two a penny in any period. . . . Art's cruel. You can get away with murder with words. But a picture is like a window straight through to your inmost heart. . . . all you've done here is build a lot of little windows to a heart full of other fashionable artists' paintings. . . . You're photographing here. That's all. (148–49)

George Paston's definition of the relationship of life to art also defines Fowles's characterization technique in *The Collector*. Miranda is a budding artist, opening herself to art and life and just learning of passion and self-expression and freedom, when she is netted by the collector–photographer Clegg, a closed being unable to feel, neurotically self-conscious yet terrified of self-definition or self-expression.

Despite the complex symbologies that Fowles creates of art and pornographic photography, of self-expression and of self-abuse (for this is what Clegg's neurotic, inferiority-obsessed mind feeds upon), and of giving and of collecting, the basic tension of this novel is a simple and classic one—the life force confronting the death force. Miranda best defines both theme and characterization when she screams in frustration:

> Do you know that every great thing in the history of art and every beautiful thing in life is actually what you call nasty or has been caused by feelings that you would call nasty? By passion, by love, by hatred, by truth. . . . Why do you take all the life out of life? Why do you kill all the beauty? (72)

Clegg never understands anything that Miranda says (Fowles's choice of an alternating relativistic narrative makes this quite clear) because he cannot and does not want to understand the terms that she uses in her attempts to express herself to him. Because of her lack of real experience, her life imitates art. Aesthetic metaphors are her only means of self-expression, and perhaps the greatest irony of the novel lies in the abject uselessness of these metaphors, which mean absolutely nothing to Clegg. Not only does Miranda die in the end because she cannot make Clegg understand that she is really sick, but throughout the novel all of her words die because they are couched in a medium that Clegg can never understand.

As the novel progresses, the frustration of her failure to communicate closes in upon Miranda as oppressively as the walls of her basement prison. First she tries to draw Clegg into the world of art—

> I started to try to explain to him. I was boasting about one of the sketches (the one I liked best). . . . It didn't mean anything to him, and he made it clear in his miserable I'll-take-your-word-for-it way that he didn't really care. . . .
> Blind, blind, other world.
> My fault, I was showing off. How could he see the magic and importance of art (not my art, of *art*) when I was so vain? (124)

—and then, in the seduction scene, which is a beautiful composition of light and shadow, she tries to draw him into the world of life. No matter how hard she tries, however, he always closes and double-locks the door between himself and any kind of human relationship with her. He is incapable of participating in emotional, aesthetic experience just as he is incapable of participating in sexual, life experience. Clegg's necrophiliac psyche, obsessed with burying the living and preserving and studying the dead, always remains encapsulated in the safety of its world of death and never ventures out into the world of life and art.

The tragedy of *The Collector* exists in the lack of communication (again mirrored in Fowles's choice of divided narratives) between the worlds of the two central characters. Miranda's artistic impulse toward freedom and light must always confront the reality of her buried-alive situation. "This crypt-room is so stuffy," she writes, "the walls squeeze in, I'm listening for him as I write, the thoughts I have are like bad drawings. Must be torn up at once" (111). Ironically, she can only express her frustration by means of artistic metaphor—

> What I write isn't natural. . . . It's the very opposite of drawing. You draw a line and you know at once whether it's a good or a bad line. But you write a line and it seems true and then you read it again later. (121)

—and for Clegg, with whom she must communicate in order to survive, metaphors are unintelligible. He cannot cope with abstractions or impressions or emotions because his mind is chained to the literal, the photographic perspective upon life.

Miranda's characterization is accomplished through her contemplation of the relationship between life and art. Clegg's characterization, however, perhaps because it is almost clinically psychological, is much more complex. The two basic concerns of Clegg's life, collecting and pornographic photography, form the image patterns whereby Fowles accomplishes Clegg's psychological characterization and defines the theme of the death of the art of life in contemporary technological society. Significantly, these two thematic image patterns do not stop with *The Collector*. Both of them reappear, in slightly altered form but carrying essentially the same thematic message, in both *The Magus* and *The French Lieutenant's Woman*.

In *The Aristos* the idea of collecting is identified as a death-directed endeavor, and collectors of all kinds are designated the carriers of the most debilitating sickness of the modern world. "My chief concern, in *The Aristos*," Fowles writes,

> is to preserve the freedom of the individual against all those pressures-to-conform that threaten our century; one of those pressures, put upon all of us, is that of labelling a person by what he gets money and fame for—by what other people most want to use him *as*. (7)

Conformity, the impulse of the mid-twentieth-century world to collect, pin, and label human beings, is an impulse nurtured daily in the armies, the corporations, and the universities. For Fowles, this is the sickness to which our century is rapidly succumbing. But even while society's institutions, the large-scale collectors, are exercising their powers of mass dehumanization, individuals also are nurturing the disease within themselves. All too often, a person tries to escape the frustration and futility of life in a world of conformity by escaping into a closed world of art. Fowles, in *The Aristos*, exposes the futility of this kind of escapism as he discusses the empty religion of the lama:

> He enjoys form rather than content; style rather than
> meaning; vogue rather than social significance; fas-
> tidiousness rather than strength. . . . He becomes a
> connoisseur, a collector . . . and all . . . of his humanity
> becomes atrophied and drops away. (112)

Thus, out of this desire to escape from the reality of life and existence into the closed but controllable world of fantasy spring forth the Cleggs of our age, gleefully flourishing their killing bottles and filling their sunless, underground rooms.

"I remember . . . G. P. saying that collectors were the worst animals of all," Miranda writes. "They're anti-life, anti-art, anti-everything" (116). "Everything free and decent in life is being locked away in filthy little cellars by beastly people who don't care" (125). Miranda's use of this image of the collector as the destroyer of vitality and beauty in the world and her allusion to her own situation in Clegg's cellar bring the novel's life–art theme vividly into focus. The image of the collector possesses great potentiality for symbolic or representational expansion. It represents all the forces in contemporary society that take away individual freedom or stifle self-expression, that force conformity by placing people and things in arbitrary categories and grouping them under general headings such as "enemy" or "subversive," and that shrink life up into the safe, closed enclaves of connoisseurs who muster under the coats of arms of their exclusive clubs, societies, and organizations. Clegg is but the extreme representation of the modern cultural diseases of conformity and exclusiveness, which are always a threat to those who try to reach the limits of the art of life.

Miranda learns from Clegg. Her character grows as her situation forces her to contemplate her own humanity. She formulates her own definition of collectordom. She rebels against the collector–force in her world when she tries to initiate Clegg into appreciation of the beauty and truth of both art and life. In turn, her self-definition and subsequent moral action fulfill her own selfhood and expand her understanding of the relation between art and life:

> Everything to do with art embarrasses him (and I suppose fascinates him). It's *all* vaguely immoral. He knows great art is great, but "great" means locked away in museums and spoken about when you want to show off. Living art, modern art shocks him. You can't talk about it with him because the word "art" starts off a whole series of shocked, guilty ideas in him. (210)

Clegg's embarrassment with art (as well as his secret fascination with it) mirrors his external embarrassment and subconscious guilty fascination with sexuality. Clegg is a collector who fears the very things that he collects. As long as he can stand back and passively contemplate the dead objects in his collection Clegg is satisfied, but when Miranda forces him to become actively involved with her—the most exquisite of the "objects" in his collection—it proves to be a very unsatisfying experience. He must restore his collection to normality and, for Clegg, normality means death.

Miranda's attitude toward collecting directly opposes Clegg's. For her, collecting is only an acceptable endeavor if it helps other human beings. She tells Clegg at one point:

> You've got to shake off the past. . . . You've got to be a new human being . . . you could collect pictures. . . . I'd introduce you to people who would tell you about art-collecting. Think of all the poor artists you could help. Instead of massacring butterflies, like a stupid schoolboy. (73)

Miranda can even humanize and give life direction to an endeavor as useless as collecting; but Clegg can never divert his idea of collecting from the ultimate direction of death.

Another obsession of Clegg's deranged psyche, his fascination with photography, adds a new dimension to the motif of collecting and gives even fuller definition to the theme of the relationship between life and art. When G. P. criticizes one of Miranda's drawings by saying, "you're photographing here," (149) his tone is openly derisive. He sees photography as mechanical, purely imitative, and literal, while art is human, original, expressive, and often abstract. The photographer is only a technician, an appendage to a machine, but the artist becomes humanly involved with his subject. The difference between photography and art is the difference between machine and man, between scientist and humanist—"I hate scientists," Miranda says, "I hate people who collect things and classify things and give them names and forget all about them. That's what people are always doing in art" (52). It is the difference between the collector (the destroyer of life) and the ecologist (the preserver and cultivator of life). When Clegg shows Miranda some of his photographs, her comments echo G. P.'s, "They're dead. . . . Not these particularly. All photos. When you draw something it lives and when you photograph it it dies" (52).

Clegg's interest in photography stems from two equally complex subconscious motives. He takes up photography as a hobby, first, to satisfy a stunted and misguided desire to be artistic, and second, to satisfy a much more complex, and more deranged, sexual desire. Clegg's first motive is pathetic because it is so unattainable. Somewhere deep within himself Clegg desires to be an artist, but because his existence is death-directed he can never participate in the experience of creation. He expresses this aesthetic desire quite early in his narrative, but his own words betray a sense of the futility of his hope. As he tries to describe Miranda's beautiful hair, he laments, "I wish I had words to describe it like a poet would or an artist" (61). Miranda senses this desire in Clegg and holds it in contempt:

> I know why he likes the photographing business. He
> thinks it makes me think he's artistic. And of course
> he hasn't a clue. I mean he gets me in focus, and that's
> all. No imagination. (131)

Clegg's photography is another form of collecting. Instead of pinning butterflies, he is capturing nature with a machine; he doesn't project any part of himself into his photographs. He doesn't try to compose his photos, or give them a special coloring, or an original perspective. He just *shoots* nature.

But Clegg's other subconscious motive for practicing photography is much more sinister, much more dehumanizing and destructive than his comparatively innocent desire to be an artist. From the very beginning, Clegg's interest in collecting and in photography is linked to his interest in pornography: Clegg is a voyeur. Unable to function sexually himself, he temporarily is satisfied with thumbing through "books of stark women." Then he graduates his voyeurism into photography. "The main idea," he writes of his taking up photography, "was to take butterflies living . . . but also often before I used to come on things out collecting, you'd be surprised the things couples get up to in places you think they would know better than to do it in, so I had that too" (13). This final addition to the motifs that define Clegg's characterization fulfills, in the terms of the novel, Clegg's role as death-directed man.

Collecting, photography, and pornography—in Fowles's novel all three motifs represent different kinds of killing, and all are different types of perversion of the life–art relationship. Pornography especially, in all of Fowles's novels, functions as a symbolic motif representing the antiexistential, dehumanizing impulse that lurks just beneath the surface of modern life and against which all moral men must rebel. Steven Marcus has noted that "pornography is opposed to literature" because literature deals "with the relations of human beings among themselves" while pornography "is not interested in persons but in organs [and] emotions are an embarrassment to it."[1] Pornography is the most antiexistential type of writing or photography because it consistently presents a dehumanized world. The pornographer turns women into objects devoid of individual personality. People are reduced to animals only capable of heeding the rutting instinct. Finally, the desire to participate in the pornographic experience verges on insanity because it is a voluntary sacrifice or denial of humanity. As Norman Mailer writes in an essay on pornography, "To put one's dream of love into the deadness of an object is to drift on the wind of the psychotic."[2]

Clegg, an embodiment of the antiexistential, pornographic impulse as defined by Steven Marcus, collects all feeling under the convenient heading of "nasty." As a pornographer he desires to deprive Miranda of her humanity and turn her into an inanimate object that he can use for the fulfillment of his unnatural sexual fantasies. In the climactic scene of *The*

1. *The Other Victorians* (London, 1966), 280.
2. *Advertisements For Myself* (New York, 1966), 396.

*Collector*, a scene that destroys any pretense of humanity in Clegg, he ties Miranda to the bed, strips her, and then takes flash pictures of her. After developing and printing these pictures, Clegg reflects that the "best ones were with her face cut off" (106). By means of pornographic photography, he succeeds in destroying Miranda's identity. In his pictures, faceless and deprived of her individual personality, Miranda has become a collection of anonymous organs as divorced from humanness as the cast-iron bed they are tied to. In headless pictures she can't talk back to him; she can no longer make him feel inferior.

This pornographic picture-taking session is the second important sexual scene in *The Collector*. In the first, Miranda tries to seduce Clegg into natural sexual intercourse. She hopes to initiate Clegg into a human relationship by means of man's and woman's basic expression of shared humanity. Clegg's sexual dysfunction and his psychological shame doom to failure Miranda's attempt to liberate his human nature. In the picture-taking scene, however, Clegg takes the initiative, and his intention is directly opposite to Miranda's in that first sexual scene. His plan to rape Miranda is the most dehumanizing kind of sexual intention because it deprives the victim of all freedom of choice.

But Clegg's rape of Miranda is even more unnatural than your normal, everyday rape. Because he is impotent, he "rapes" her with his camera, his own peculiar version of a mechanical dildo. In Michaelangelo Antonioni's film, *Blow-up*, a similar point about the unnatural intrusion of the machine into the natural, sexual life of identity-deprived modern man is made in an early scene in which the photographer–protagonist "makes love" to his model with his camera. For Fowles and Antonioni, the depersonalization of sexuality is one indicator that the mid-twentieth-century dependence on technology is bringing an increasingly dark age into the history of the art of life. A dramatic adaptation by David Parker of *The Collector*, which played in London in 1971 and 1972, brilliantly—and, for the audience, perhaps uncomfortably—captured Fowles's meaning in this dehumanizing scene.[3] As Clegg began to shoot, a brutal strobe light pierced the dimness of the stage and began rhythmically, faster and faster and harder and harder, to assault with pounding shafts of light the tableau of Miranda tied to the bed while Clegg prowled the shadows excitedly caressing his camera. Finally, the scene, and the audience, dropped into exhausted darkness. The mechanical orgasm had been attained and what had approximated a human world had been transformed into an eerie, oppressive, fragmented world of unnatural light and sinister shadows. The whole dramatic experience left an unhealthy taste in the mouth of the audience; the kind of taste, perhaps, that one might get from eating a clockwork orange.

As his obsessive desire to take pornographic photographs rises, Clegg tries to justify his perversion by invoking the name of "art." The day before the mechanical rape, he had asked Miranda to pose naked for photographs that he supposedly could use as a deterrent to keep her from telling the police about him after he released her. "Not obscene" pictures, he says, simply "photos you wouldn't want published. Art-photographs" (102). His idea of art-photography evidently comes from reading magazines like

3. The play was first produced at The King's Head Theatre Club in Islington and then at The Shepherd's Bush Theatre Club in Shepherd's Bush Green.

> *Shoes* with very interesting pictures of girls, mainly
> their legs, wearing different sorts of shoes, some just
> shoes and belts, they were really unusual pictures,
> artistic. (103)

But pornography, especially photographs of headless organs randomly adorned with shoes or belts or taut ropes, can never be artistic because it devalues the living, the human, the free, and it exalts the disembodied, the dehumanized, the depraved. Miranda adamantly refuses to allow Clegg to apply the concept of art to his pornographic intentions for her. She screams:

> You disgusting filthy mean-minded bastard. . . . You're
> breaking every decent human law, every decent human
> relationship, every decent thing that's ever happened
> between your sex and mine. (102–3)

In *The Collector*, pornography's crime is not against the "public good" or the "innocent child," but is against art, which is symbolically synonymous with life. Pornography for Fowles is an existential crime, and when Clegg cuts off Miranda's head in his photographs he might as well be decapitating her with an ax. He is hacking away her identity and humanity, destroying the art of her life.

Thus, the images of collecting, of photography, and of pornography come together to define the art–life theme. By the end of the novel, the veteran collector Clegg is well on the way to becoming a connoisseur of pornographic photographs. Already he is considering kidnapping another girl, "just . . . for the interest of the thing and to compare them" (225). He doesn't want to compare the girls, however; he wants to compare his porno–pictures of the girls. Clegg becomes like the fiend in the old horror film, *House of Wax*, who abducts beautiful women, kills them, and then covers their bodies with boiling wax in order to make the most artistic and true-to-life figures to populate his wax museum. He is an unscrupulous collector who perverts art by destroying life.

The symbolic motifs of collecting and of pornographic photography, which Fowles introduces in his first novel, *The Collector*, also appear in *The Magus* and *The French Lieutenant's Woman*. And, in both of these later novels, these motifs help to define Fowles's theme of life imitating art. Nicholas Urfe, the protagonist of *The Magus*, is in many ways like Frederick Clegg. All his life Nicholas has been a collector of women. He looks at them, handles them, acquires them, but he never establishes a human relationship with any of them. He is "always careful to make sure that the current victim knew, before she took her clothes off, the difference between coupling and marrying" (17). Alison, through her intense powers of perception, recognizes immediately Nicholas's inability to become involved. "You're the *affaire de peau* type" she says. "You're already thinking, how the hell am I going to get rid of this stupid Australian slut" (25). But it is left to another extremely perceptive woman much later in *The Magus* to make the kinship of Frederick Clegg and Nicholas Urfe explicit. Lily de Seitas, by Fowles's own admission a female magus figure,[4] charges that Nicholas fell in love with Lily as "an unscrupulous collector falls in love with a painting he wants" (550). But of course, unlike Clegg, Nicholas is sane. He is still tractable, possessing the potentiality for being educated out of his collector–consciousness.

Nicholas's mentor who will lead him out of collector–consciousness and into a new moral self-aware-

4. *Afterwords: Novelists on Their Novels* (New York, 1969), 172.

**44**

ness is Conchis, the magus. And Conchis's pedagogy is quite simple: He forces Nicholas's life to imitate art. By means of artistic creation, often simple story-telling, he demonstrates to Nicholas the desirability of rebellion against collector–consciousness. Conchis tells the story of his own life in hopes that Nicholas will be able to identitfy with its lessons. One of the major lessons of Conchis's life was taught him by Henrik, the prophet of Seidevarre. Conchis tells of the realization

> that my whole approach was scientific, medical, clas-
> sifying. I was conditioned by a kind of ornithological
> approach to man. I thought in terms of species, behaviors,
> observations. . . . I knew the man out there on the
> point was having an experience beyond the scope of
> all my science and reason, and I knew my science and
> reason would always be defective until they could
> comprehend what was happening in Henrik's mind. (287)

From this first realization of his own collector–con-sciousness Conchis saw that

> the attempt to scientize reality, to name it and classify
> it and vivisect it out of existence, was like trying to
> remove all the air from atmosphere. In the creating of
> the vacuum it was the experimenter who died, because
> he was inside the vacuum. . . . I was to look for the
> water, not the wave. (370–71)

Conchis's point is that the collector–scientist–cata-loguer, destroys his own humanity when he refuses to relate emotionally and naturally to his fellow man.

The poetic image of the water and the wave, since art in the Fowles world interprets life best, defines Conchis's realization of the necessity for unity and flux, for freedom and involvement, both within indi-vidual man and among all men. Conchis first received the image from one of his existential mentors, and he in turn passes it along to Nicholas. De Deukans was a collector, "he had devoted his whole life to this collecting of collections," but he did not collect things in order to kill them. He collected priceless musical instruments in order to bring his château alive with beautiful music. He collected pieces of classical architecture and countless *objets d'art* in the attempt to create an ambience in which he could exist. Conchis describes De Deukans's success in the uniting of the worlds of art and life in terms that once again call up memories of Oscar Wilde. "It was unnatural, of course," Conchis tells Nicholas. "But all dandyism and eccentricity is more or less unnatural in a world dominated by the desperate struggle for economic survival" (172). Conchis also realizes, however, that De Deukans was too much like Oscar Wilde, that he finally succumbed to the decadence that falsifies the life–art relationship. It is "true of all collecting," Conchis says. "It extinguishes the moral instinct. The object finally possesses the possessor" (174).

And yet, De Deukans, like Wilde, was a poet and his legacy to Conchis was an image in the form of an existential question:

*Ultram bibis*? *Aquam an undam*? Which are you drinking? The water or the wave? (183)

This poetic aspect, absent in Clegg, finally is what redeems De Deukans's decadent collector–consciousness. It gives some meaning to his life and it goes on giving meaning in the future to the lives of Conchis and Nicholas. Just as Yeats in the last two lines of *Among School Children*—

O body swayed to music, O brightening glance, How can we know the dancer from the dance?

—found hope in the movement and vitality of man uniting with the art of the dance to affirm the value of life, so does Conchis hope that Nicholas will cast off the scarecrow essence of his collector–consciousness and immerse his new existence in the symbolic water of life. A collector tries to separate the dancer from the dance, the wave from the water, and because the two are inseparable he succeeds only in destroying both, and the moving world of life comes to a standstill, dries up. Separating the water from the wave is like cutting the head off of Miranda's body; all beauty, life, and meaning dies.

Another part of Conchis's education of Nicholas involves teaching him to reject, as unnatural and dehumanizing, the pornographic impulse that exists in all men. At times Conchis delivers this specific lesson with wry and subtle humor, such as when he leaves the magazine entitled *The Beauties of Nature* in Nicholas's bedroom:

> The nature was all female, and the beauty all pectoral. There were long shots of breasts, shots of breasts of every material from every angle, and against all sorts of backgrounds, closer and closer, until the final picture was of nothing but breast, with one dark and much larger than natural nipple staring from the center of the glossy page. It was much too obsessive to be erotic. (97–98)

This is pornography photographed à la Clegg, headless, even bodiless, and its effect is comic because it is, despite the magazine's title, unnatural, cut off from even the approximation of anything human. At other times, however, Conchis's lessons about the pornographic impulse are not nearly so funny, but rather brutal and sadistic, delivered with unmitigated realism.

Conchis's "disintoxication" of Nicholas from the godgame consists specifically of a visual explanation which Nicholas has absolutely no choice but to accept, of the great difference between man's pornographic impulse and the art of life. Conchis makes his point by handcuffing Nicholas to a wall and juxtaposing before his eyes, which he cannot close, a pornographic "blue movie" and a living work of art, an intensely human literary scene. Conchis's disintoxication of Nicholas is similar to the disintoxication from sex and ultraviolence of Anthony Burgess's antihero, Alex, in *A Clockwork Orange*. Like Alex, bound and "choiceless" (468), Nicholas must undergo the "metaphorical, if not . . . literal, flogging," (469) of Conchis's pornography. The film is composed of a succession of dislocated anatomical parts:

a naked leg ending in a foot in a high-heeled black shoe resting on his stomach. . . . It could easily have been any white woman's leg; and any black man's stomach and hands. (473)
An anonymous white hand stroked an anonymous phallus. (474)

Nicholas passively watches and acknowledges the ridiculousness of this succession of jerky images of disembodied organs until, near the end, he sees himself and Alison in the movie. He is shocked—the clip is of their weekend on Mount Parnassus and he wonders if their lovemaking by the secluded pool has been filmed—because, in a sense, this last section of the film is the most pornographic part of all. During that weekend Nicholas was using Alison's body, exploiting her emotions in order to bolster his own ego. Like the director of a quickie porno movie, Nicholas spent the weekend hustling his model from one scene to another, imposing upon her his false image of reality, and then unemotionally packing her off at the end—"Wham! Bam! Thank you, ma'am!" Ironically, however, unbeknownst to Nicholas, a porno movie was all the time being made of the making of his porno movie. And in the end Conchis turns all of Nicholas's own inhumanity back upon him.

But Nicholas's disintoxication does not end with the realization of the pornographic impulse within his own personality. Conchis goes on to demonstrate, by means of a visual juxtaposition, just how divorced from the real art of life Nicholas's life of pornographic exploitation is. Conchis follows his jerky, blurred, poorly filmed "blue movie" with an exquisite work of living art that draws upon both visual and literary reference for its meaning. This living painting–drama captures all the expressive beauty of Goya's *Maja Desnuda* combined with the powerful emotion of the Othello–Desdemona love relationship. And all the time Nicholas is cut off from the art of life—Iago hung on the wall, master manipulator of the lives of others with no concern for human emotion or love. As he watches the painting come to life and notes the naturalness of the sexuality, the point of Conchis's simple juxtaposition penetrates the thickness of his egocentricity:

> There was no perversion, no attempt to suggest that I was watching anything else but two people who were in love making love. . . . He was tender with her, she was tender with him, and they behaved as if to show that the reality was the very antithesis of the absurd nastiness of the film. (477)

Perhaps for a moment he forgets that he is part of the "absurd nastiness" of the blue movie, but he soon realizes that the difference between the pornographic film and the living painting is the same as the difference between his false relationship with Alison and the true art of living and loving. The living painting represents the real beauty that exists in life, while the blue movie represents the meaningless lives that so many modern men seem content to create for themselves. Conchis is telling Nicholas to stop collecting pornographic relationships and to begin to imitate art.

The thematic motifs of collecting and pornography in *The French Lieutenant's Woman* function in almost exactly the same manner and to the same end as in Fowles's first two novels. Charles Smithson, in one of his more pompous moments, declares to his fiancée Ernestina, "you forget that I'm a scientist. I have written a monograph so I must be" (12–13). Charles is a scientist much as Clegg is a scientist. Where Clegg collects butterflies, Charles collects fossils and, like Clegg, is fascinated by beauty dead, by past life frozen in rock. Charles pretends to be a Darwinist and yet he is very much drawn to

> the Linnaean *Scala Naturae*, the ladder of nature, whose great keystone . . . was *nulla species nova*: a new species cannot enter the world. This principle explains the Linnaean obsession with classifying and naming, with fossilizing the existent. We can see it now as a foredoomed attempt to stabilize and fix what is in reality a continuous flux, and it seems highly appropriate that Linnaeus himself finally went mad. (45)

Charles is certainly a collector, like Clegg and like Linnaeus, but unlike them he does not go mad. Charles is, as was Nicholas Urfe, still tractable, still educable.

In a sense, both *The Magus* and *The French Lieutenant's Woman* are *Bildungsromane* while *The Collector* is an attempted *Bildungsroman* that fails because the student, Clegg, is incapable of learning. *The French Lieutenant's Woman* is the story of how Charles

Smithson is taught by his mentor, Sarah, to rebel against the classifying and fossilizing impulse of the Victorian Age. Just as Conchis teaches Nicholas to reject the pornographic impulse to use women and then cast them off, Sarah teaches Charles that human relationships cannot always be neatly classified and then filed away for future reference like the fossils in his collection. Charles wants to dehumanize his relationship with Sarah and turn it, as Dr. Grogan would, into a neatly labeled psychological "case" (134), but he cannot:

> Moments like modulations come in human relationships: when what has been until then an objective situation, one perhaps described by the mind to itself in semi-literary terms, one it is sufficient to classify under some general heading . . . becomes subjective; becomes unique; becomes, by empathy, instantaneously shared rather than observed. (115)

Just as Nicholas could not edge the death of Alison into the realm of aesthetics, Charles Smithson, though he tried to "look at Sarah as an object of his past" (153), cannot find any handy cubicle in which to file her. Sarah is this novel's magus who will, perhaps, lead Charles out of the collector–consciousness of the Victorian Age and into a timeless world of selfhood.

Sarah, if he will allow her, can save Charles from becoming like George Eliot's Casaubon, who spent his life in musty libraries collecting fragments of the past, labeling them, and filing them away for future reference in a book never to be completed. Casaubon's death, from the fossilization of his heart in fatty tissue, symbolizes the atrophy of feeling that became a common disease in the Victorian Age. If *The French Lieutenant's Woman* had ended in Chapter forty-four, Charles would have been doomed to live out the life

of a Casaubon, unself-conscious and fostering the Lin-
naean attitude of "fossilizing the existent." But the
book does go on and Sarah does lead Charles to an
awareness of the "priority of existence over death, of
the individual over the species, of ecology over classi-
fication" (192).

One of the steps on Charles's journey to awareness that Sarah Woodruff does not control involves
Charles's investigation of the pornographic alternative
to natural sexual life. Just as Fowles used the juxtaposition of pornography to reality with such telling effect
in *The Magus*, so also does he juxtapose Charles's
descent into the underbelly of Victorian England, the
drunken trip to Ma Terpsichore's Haymarket brothel,
to the reality of Charles's brief relationship with the
young prostitute who is so appropriately named Sarah.
Fowles makes, as he does in *The Magus*, the opposition
between pornography and real human relationship
quite explicit. Even scientific, oft-insensitive Charles
realizes that the "individual" Sarah (both of them) is
something quite different from the easily dismissible
"species," London *whore*.

Charles and his two compatriots leave their exclusive club and head for the Haymarket where "the
evening's talent," which consists of women who have
given up their identities, parades "dressed as Parisian
bargees . . . as sailors, as senoritas, as Sicilian peasant
girls" (238–39). They enter Ma Terpsichore's famous
whorehouse and they witness scenes that have "probably changed less in the course of history than those
of any other human activity" (239). But Fowles does
not describe those scenes in detail as the skin-book
writer would, nor does he lingeringly focus upon their
perversion as the porno moviemaker would; rather, he

quotes a passage from a genuine work of pornography, "originally published in 1749, the same year as Cleland's masterpiece in the genre, *Fanny Hill*" (240). Thus, he uses an attempt at art, dead as it may be, to describe life, dead as it is. As the scenes of perversion unfold before him, Charles, unlike his companions, finds himself reluctant to join in the pornographic spirit of the evening:

> The white bodies embraced, contorted, mimicked; but it seemed to Charles that there was a despair behind the fixed suggestive smiles of the performers. One was a child who could only just have reached puberty; and there seemed in her assumption of demure innocence something genuinely virginal, still agonized, not fully hardened by her profession. (242)

He is personalizing what should be impersonal, individualizing what can be classified simply as group perversion.

Charles leaves this gathering of pornographers—the girls, bound to their lives as prostitutes, striking poses according to the directions of their customers, are victims like Miranda, forced to pose for a succession of Cleggs without cameras—and picks up a young prostitute named Sarah with whom he spends the rest of the evening. Charles's brief relationship with this young woman and her infant child comprises the second half of Fowles's juxtaposition of pornography to reality. And this scene in the prostitute's rooms has, like its precursor, the living painting in *The Magus*, its literary echoes. The events of Charles's evening with Sarah the prostitute directly parallel the events described in Dante Gabriel Rossetti's poem "Jenny." Like Rossetti with his Jenny, Charles cannot exploit this Sarah, cannot make her suffer

from the hatefulness of man,
Who spares not to end what he began,
Whose acts are ill and his speech ill,
Who, having used you at his will,
Thrusts you aside, as when I dine
I serve the dishes and the wine. (from "Jenny")

Fowles is being ironically playful in conjuring up this particular literary echo; considering that the novel actually ends, twice, in the home of Dante Gabriel Rossetti. He is also, however, being quite serious. Charles cannot exploit this young whore, as his companions are exploiting the other whores, because he knows too much about her. He cannot deny her humanity; he cannot violate the natural love that she (and he himself) shows for the child. The personalization of his relationship to this Sarah makes possible the personalization of his relationship to Sarah Woodruff.

In each of these novels, Fowles uses the themes of collecting and of pornography to represent man's socially cultivated talent for dehumanization. Pornography is Fowles's ultimate symbol of loss of identity and the obscenity of the destruction of human selfhood. Each Fowles novel builds to a climactic scene which demonstrates the difference between pornography and humanity. In existential terms, the ideas of collecting and of pornography are intense expressions of "object consciousness." The collector and the pornographer are intent upon turning living things into objects that can be used, exploited, and controlled according to the owner's whim. Fowles is writing about collector–pornographers like Mrs. Poulteney "in the first possessive pleasure of her new toy" (55), Sarah; or Mr. Freeman, happily closing "an excellent business deal" (71), his daughter's marriage. In each of his

54

novels Fowles, in concert with his use of the idea of pornography as a symbolic motif, shows the exploitation of women by male pornographers. In his consistent returning to this theme he is demonstrating the need to overthrow the pornographic law according to which women "are to sit . . . like so many articles in a shop and to let . . . men walk in and turn them over and point at this one or that one—*she* takes my fancy" (310). But Fowles is not writing only about female emancipation; he is also writing in favor of the emancipation of the collectors and the pornographers from their destiny. As his novels so often demonstrate, the collector is as imprisoned, is missing as much, as his victim; the pornographer is as dehumanized as his object. Fowles makes this thematic construct most clear by choosing a statement from Marx as the epigraph for *The French Lieutenant's Woman*:

> *Every emancipation is a restoration of the human world and of human relationships to man himself.*

Fowles wants his readers to realize the necessity of freeing themselves from the collector–pornographer consciousness of the modern world.

The motifs of collecting and pornography, however, are not Fowles's only means of exhibiting his "life-imitates-art" theme in *The Magus* and *The French Lieutenant's Woman*. In both of these novels the life–art theme functions with much more variety than in *The Collector*. For example, the life–art theme is especially evident in the descriptive style of *The Magus*, whereas *The Collector* is not really a stylish novel at all. While *The Magus* and *The French Lieutenant's Woman* are always lushly descriptive, the style of *The Collector* is generally stark and clipped and hurried because that is the nature of the situation that is being described. Also, Fowles's choice in *The Collector* of alternating first-person narratives, one composed by a minimally educated, nonverbal madman and the other composed in the form of hurried, surreptitious diary entries, dictates the use of a starkly realistic style. In contrast, *The Magus* is a novel of slowly unfolding events and the narrator, Nicholas, who likes to think of himself as a poet, finds great pleasure in presenting elaborate descriptions couched in a style liberally sprinkled with poetic similes and metaphors. And, the omniscient narrator of *The French Lieutenant's Woman* recreates the grand style of the high Victorian novelists, a style renowned for its leisure, its minute detailing of events, and its unmatched powers of animated description. Whereas in *The Collector* the life–art theme is defined in terms of the movement of abstract ideas—collecting and pornography—into the realm of thematic symbolism, in *The Magus* and *The French Lieutenant's Woman* the life–art theme is continually revealed in the style.

The style of *The Magus* is generated out of specific kinds of similes and metaphors. The narrator's similes are almost exclusively drawn from the world of art—painting and literature—and the central metaphor of the novel is based upon the premise that the world is a living theater, populated with playwrights, actors, and an audience, in which the art of life is dramatized. The narrator's similes in *The Magus*, his ever-present aesthetic analogies, are the most direct expressions in Fowles's fiction of the manner in which life imitates art.

At times, reading *The Magus* is more like wandering through an art gallery than through the world of a novel. People and scenes become pictures, and the reality, which is sometimes quite beautiful, sometimes quite horrible, is aesthetically distanced. Henry James's famous Lambinet scene in *The Ambassadors* accomplishes this descriptive interweaving of life and art, and Fowles, whose appreciation of great painting is obvious and whose understanding of art is acute, repeatedly tries for that same Jamesian effect. Lily, Nicholas's elusive lover in Conchis's masque, undergoes a number of aesthetic transfigurations in Nicholas's eyes. When he first sees her coming out of Conchis's study, she is only an anonymous girl in "some genre picture—The Secret. The Admonition" (151). But later, on the beach, she looks "like a Renoir" (188), while much later, standing naked before him, she becomes "Botticelli's Primavera" (433). Other characters in Conchis's masque seem, to Nicholas, to have stepped off of famous canvasses. Nicholas's vision of Robert Foulkes, the seventeenth-century murderer, is "a Rembrandt, disturbingly authentic" (136), and the face of the De Deukans figure whom he meets in the street outside the Hotel Philadelphia is "as gloomy as an El Greco" (156). The landscapes and scenes of *The Magus* also exhibit the distinctive colorings of specific artists. The scene of a Nazi execution, "as monstrous as Goya etchings" (319), is contrasted to the green beauty of "a Dufy day" (401), while on a moonless, cloudy night Nicholas describes "a gray Palmeresque light over the landscape" (423).

But Nicholas's aesthetic similes are not all from painting, many are literary. Besides being a Renoir–Botticelli–Beardsley beauty, Lily is "like a heroine in Chekhov, unpredictable, shifting, always prey to something beyond the words and moods of the apparent situation" (271) or moves "Virginia Woolf-like" (330) before Nicholas's eyes. In the Norwegian woman, Ragnar, Conchis sees a "tragic dimension";

she has "Euripidean eyes" and lives in "pure Strind-bergian melancholia" (280). Her brother, Henrik, the god-seeking hermit, has carved biblical texts on the ceiling of his cabin that remind Conchis of the quotations on the ceiling of Montaigne's study, but the room has "none of the sanity of Montaigne. . . . More the intensity of Pascal's famous *Memorial*" (282). Nicholas also describes his experiences in literary terms. His fake suicide attempt early in the novel was "not a moral action, but a fundamentally aesthetic one. . . . It was a Mercutio death I was looking for, not a real one" (58).

Nicholas and Conchis repeatedly use these aesthetic similes because this kind of description distances one momentarily from the reality of a person or a scene. Nicholas especially is always trying to escape from reality. Only when he is confronted by intensely real works of art does he stop exploiting art and start seeing its human significance. Costly art works hang impressively or stand at attention in each room of Conchis's villa—a Modigliani woman with simian eyes, Rodin and Giacometti sculptures, and two exquisite Bonnard nudes. At different times, these art works seem alive to Nicholas; "The Modigliani seemed to glare at me severely" (100), he thinks one evening as he prowls Conchis's villa. The paintings, the literature, the other works of art at Bourani seem more real than the rather mystifying reality—or *réalités*—that Nicholas experiences there. Bourani itself is an imitation of art—when Nicholas sees "Fra Angelico's famous *Annunciation*" in one of Conchis's art books he realizes "why the colonnade outside had seemed so familiar. There was even the same white-edged floor of red tiles" (90). The world of art that Conchis propels Nicholas into fosters a kind of sensitivity training. For

Nicholas, the Bonnard nude is "an unforgettable painting" that sets "a dense golden halo of light round the most trivial of moments, so that the moment, and all such moments, could never be completely trivial again" (93). Nicholas finally thinks of the Bonnard that it "was the reality; such moments" (95), little realizing that as the masque, the godgame, slowly unfolds he will be experiencing a whole succession of those special moments when art becomes reality.

Conchis intentionally creates this aesthetic ambience in order to jar Nicholas out of a limited and egocentric conception of reality and into a world of larger, more meaningful *réalités*. Throughout the novel Conchis uses art as a stimulant to consciousness, a hypo to introspection. He even looks like Picasso, "quintessential Mediterranean man, who had discarded everything that lay between him and his vitality" (78). Conchis envisions himself as an artist of life, one of the elite who has passed through his apprenticeship to become a *maestro* responsible for growth in others. He bombards Nicholas with aesthetic stimuli and, because his student is extremely receptive, a deeper consciousness begins to appear. Nicholas tells how "the first time I . . . heard him play great music . . . I was moved as I had been by the Bonnards. . . . I was experiencing . . . a new self-acceptance . . . an awareness of a new kind of potentiality" (159). Stimulation to self-consciousness is Conchis's existential game. His concept of art is straightforwardly Platonic. Art should both entertain and instruct, and the decor of Conchis's world aims at teaching life to imitate art, teaching Nicholas to interpret, react to, and finally join the existential godgame.

Conchis's real aesthetic flair, however, is for drama. He turns Bourani and the surrounding area into a large and highly versatile stage. And he tells Nicholas of

> a new kind of drama. One in which the conventional relations between audience and actors were forgotten. In which the conventional scenic geography, the notions of proscenium, stage, auditorium, were completely discarded. In which continuity of performance, either in time or place, was ignored. And in which the action, the narrative was fluid, with only a point of departure and a fixed point of conclusion. . . . You will find that Artaud and Pirandello and Brecht were all thinking in their different ways along similar lines. But they had neither the money nor the will—and perhaps not the time—to think as far as I did. The element that they could never bring themselves to discard was the audience. . . . Here we are all actors. . . . I am an actor too, Nicholas, in this strange new meta-theatre. (366–67)

Lionel Abel in his book entitled *Metatheatre*, which deals with such playwrights as Pirandello and Brecht, defines metaplays as "theatre pieces about life seen as already theatricalized" and notes that this kind of theater almost invariably employs some form of the play-within-a-play technique.[5] Conchis's ongoing metatheatrical experiment is the most prominent art work within this art work; his elaborately mounted play-within-a-novel has the same intention and is meant to produce the same effect as the play-within-a-play in what Lionel Abel calls the archetypal work of metatheater, Shakespeare's *Hamlet*. In staging his play-within-the-novel Conchis is adding a third intention to the Platonic definitions of the purpose of art, which he had affirmed earlier. He is saying that art must delight and surely it must instruct, but also it must involve.

5. *Metatheatre: A New View of Dramatic Form* (New York, 1963), 60.

Art must draw human life into aesthetic consciousness and, subsequently, participation. Conchis's whole intention in mounting his elaborate play-within-a-novel is first, to seduce Nicholas into enjoyment of the unique theater experiment that is being performed only for him; second, to teach Nicholas of the eternally expanding possibilities for moral action and moral choice that exist in the life of every human being; and finally, to encourage Nicholas to enter into the play, place his own mind and body into dramatized situations in which he must make moral choices, and then correlate those choices to physical action.

As the masque begins, Nicholas is a "solitary audience of one" (138) in the "now uncurtained theatre" (354) and Conchis immediately assumes the role of the omnipotent dramatist in control of every scene, every person, every aspect of his production. As Nicholas notes on only his second visit to Bourani:

> Underlying everything he did I had come to detect an air of stage management, of the planned and rehearsed. He did not tell me of his coming to Bourani as a man tells something that chances to occur to him, but far more as a dramatist tells an anecdote where the play requires. (105)

Not only does Conchis write the script, direct, and narrate his masque; he also casts, choreographs, costumes, handles set design, engineers the special effects, and even furnishes musical accompaniment, all in addition to acting one of the leading roles.

Perhaps Conchis the dramatist demonstrates his imaginative genius most distinctively in his handling of the backstage duties of casting director and wardrobe manager. Having written a complex drama involving *Doppelgänger* effects, literary allusions to *Othello*, and the reincarnation of Nazi sadists, Conchis assembles a professional repertory company that can effectively act all of the difficult roles. This company also, in accordance with Conchis's conception of meta-theater, can intelligently improvise in accordance with the many spontaneous script changes dictated by the "living drama." Often, he costumes his repertory company in garb available in any theatrical wardrobe—Nazi uniforms, a black Puritan frock coat, high-necked Victorian dresses—but at other times, such as when he brings a pack of Tarot cards to life, or when he choreographs a mythological allegory, he demonstrates his genius for surrealistic, avant-garde, symbolic costuming. Even the design of a simple sundress in an "*art nouveau*" style is, to Nicholas, "as arresting as a brilliant stage costume" (267). Every costume that Conchis designs gives symbolic punctuation to the scene in which it is worn.

Conchis is also always aware of the lighting of his masque. Before each narrative block of his own life story and before each dramatic scene, he modulates the lighting to fit the mood or directs light so as to illuminate specific aspects of the masque. He is continually turning out the lights or dimming them or moving lamps so as to illuminate only specific areas of the verandah. For example, immediately after intoning, "We come from night, we go into night. Why live in night?" (122), Conchis plunges the verandah into pitch darkness and then narratively tumbles Nicholas into the trenches of World War I. At another time, Nicholas notices that "the lamp had been put behind me so that it would light her entrance; and it was an entrance to take the breath away" (163). Conchis repeatedly creates, especially in terms of lighting, the typical Conradian verandah situation—two men, the old, experienced tale-teller and his silent auditor, sitting opposite each other in a darkness pierced only by a steady, speaking voice and, perhaps, the red tracer of a lighted cigarette.

Conchis also uses music to create mood. He plays Bach as an overture to his introduction of Lily to Nicholas and to his mythological, dramatic allegory of Apollo, Artemis–Diana, and the satyr that is the grand production number of that evening. He floods the hills with the martial strains of "Tipperary" in order to conjure images of World War I in Nicholas's mind and, late at night, he lures Nicholas with harpsi-chord music out of bed and into a first brief glimpse of Lily. Each event that occurs during Nicholas's visit to Bourani becomes a brilliant *"coup de théâtre"* (271) and Conchis, the omnipotent playwright–director of it all, displays "that great dramatic skill, the art of tim-ing" (206).

In fact, Conchis's masque is staged so profession-ally that inevitably Nicholas feels the desire to get in-volved, to leave behind his role as "audience of one" and to participate as an actor in the living drama: "It was a masque, and I wanted, or after a very short while began to want, to play my part" (165). He begins to view Conchis as being "like some European nobleman. We were his Earl of Leicester's troupe, his very private company" (334–35). However, as the novel progresses and the scenes of the play-within-a-novel are linked and the motifs developed, Nicholas realizes that Con-chis is staging more than a private masque. The meta-theatrical play artistically represents the bigger play in which we "are all actors and actresses" on the vast "stage of the world" (170).

Since many of the scenes in Conchis's play are later replayed in Nicholas's own life, Fowles's theme of life imitating art is most fully defined in the characterization of Conchis as a dramatic artist and in the meta-theatrical situation that Conchis creates. The whole intention behind Conchis's professionally mounted metaplay is to bring together the worlds of art and life. Early in the novel, Nicholas rejects the moral, human responsibilities of life, first by running away from Alison to Phraxos and then by considering suicide. Conchis hopes to entice Nicholas into active participation in the metaplay—a type of involvement that Nicholas initially rejects as he seems content to sit passively as the bemused audience of one. Conchis's real intention surfaces only later. When the metaplay ends and real life begins, Conchis hopes that Nicholas will sustain the meticulously rehearsed role of existentially responsible man in that more important drama, the drama of life. Conchis tries to explain to Nicholas how metatheater integrates art and life—"No good play has a real curtain, Nicholas. It is acted, and then it continues to act" (402)—but the life–art relationship moves out of potentiality and into actuality if Nicholas chooses to apply the lessons he has learned in the metaplay to the action of his own life.

Conchis's metatheatrical play fully lives up to Fowles's declaration in *The Aristos* that "good art seeks to provoke mystery" (153). Nicholas spends the final third of the novel playing the role of a literary detective trying to solve the many mysteries provoked by the play. One of the most important thematic statements in *The Magus* occurs when Conchis tells Nicholas that he envies him because "You have the one thing that matters. You have all your discoveries before you" (79). For an existentially conscious man, art is discovery, drama is discovery, and life is an endless flux of discoveries. Conchis, an omniscient artist who lives inside the world of the novel, is a persona for the novelist himself; Nicholas is the reading audience, existentially unconscious man, that Fowles the novelist is trying to delight, instruct, and involve by means of his art. Just as Conchis hopes to lead his "audience of one" to the discovery of self, so also does Fowles, by means of an open ending, hope to entice his readers into participation in solving the mystery of his novel. He wants his readers to see the relevance of this particular work of art, *The Magus*, to their own lives. Fowles, in *The Magus*, is examining the fundamental relationship between the artist and his audience. He is dramatizing a new theory of participatory art, a theory that he defines much more fully in his next novel, *The French Lieutenant's Woman*.

At first reading, Fowles's third novel seems to be another existential novel in which the protagonists, Charles Smithson and Sarah Woodruff, attempt to find selfhood in a world which represses individuality. Beneath this human theme, however, *The French Lieutenant's Woman* is really about art. In a sense, it is the most creative kind of literary criticism. It personifies the past of the novel as genre while simultaneously probing the modern atrophy of the genre. It examines the style and tradition of the genre's past, not in imitation of that past, but rather as a means of breaking the bonds of tradition. Fowles's intrusive commentaries in *The French Lieutenant's Woman* on the genre of the novel are a plea for art to imitate life; a plea for the genre to rebel, as Smithson is given the opportunity to do, against the tyranny of the past and find identity in new experimental forms.

In *The Magus*, Fowles prefigures the aesthetic theme of *The French Lieutenant's Woman*. "The novel is dead," Conchis says in one of his earliest conversations with Nicholas. "Why should I struggle through hundreds of pages of fabrication to reach half a dozen very little truths? . . . Words are for truth. For Facts. Not Fiction." And, handing Nicholas an old, dusty pamphlet *"Containing the Last Words of the Murderer Robert Foulkes,"* he challenges Nicholas to "see if it is not more real than all the historical novels you have ever read" (92–93). Conchis's strong aversion to the novel genre, and his despair of that genre ever being of any human value, has grown out of the conviction that the novel as a genre has progressively lost touch with real life. Conchis as artist, therefore, being a man who had once written a novel (which he subsequently burned), turns away from the novel to metatheater to satisfy his demands for a living art form. Ironically, despite the objections of his persona to historical novels, Fowles goes on to write exactly that. *The French Lieutenant's Woman* is a historical novel, but it is one laced with a truly contemporary aesthetic theme.

Fowles, the artist behind the artist in *The Magus*, seems to share Conchis's aversion to the novel genre of the past, but he does not share Conchis's despair in the novel's potential vitality as an art form. In his essay about the composition of *The French Lieutenant's Woman*, Fowles tells how his experience on a movie set causes

> a re-affirmation in my faith in the novel. For all its faults, it is a statement by one person. In my novels I am producer, director and all the actors; I photograph it. . . . There *is* a vanity about it, a wish to play the godgame. . . . The truth is, the novel is a free form. Unlike the play or the filmscript, it has no limits other than those of the language. It is like a poem; it can be what it wants.[6]

6. *Afterwords: Novelists on Their Novels*, 169–70.

Fowles believes that just as men and women like Charles Smithson and Sarah Woodruff can be free to exist, so also can the novel, that "free form," be a living and existential art form.

Writing a novel is, in fact, like taking part in the godgame. As long as everyone involved—the novelist, the characters, the reader—is capable of acting freely, then the novel can come alive. At one point in *The Magus* Nicholas actually characterizes Conchis as a "novelist *sans* novel, creating with people, not words" (229). Later, Nicholas envisions himself as a novelist and begins to understand the meaning of Conchis's pronunciations about dead art forms:

> All my life I had tried to turn life into fiction, to hold reality away; always I had acted as if a third person was watching and listening and giving me marks for good or bad behaviour—a god like a novelist, to whom I turned like a character with the power to please, the sensitivity to feel slighted, the ability to adapt himself to whatever he believed the novelist–god wanted. (487)

This particular novelist, Nicholas, can write only dead novels because he has cut his real life off from his art and has taken away the freedom of his central character, his living self. His life, which he orchestrates at arm's length, is merely a dead novel. As a novelist–god he imposes an essence upon his central character, himself, and thus that character cannot exist. Nicholas the novelist is creating exactly the kind of dead, false art that Conchis has described, and ironically Nicholas's dead novel is also his dead life.

Just as both Conchis and Nicholas bring art and life together and find new freedom in the union, *The French Lieutenant's Woman* is also an exercise in metatheater, though its emphases are much different. In his third novel Fowles becomes the Conchis-like novelist–

god but then, happily he abdicates that antiexistential role as Conchis does also. He creates in *The French Lieutenant's Woman* a dramatic situation in which the reading audience can enter into the fictional world, participate in the events of that world, and even resolve those events. At the end of this novel Fowles jauntily enters his waiting coach and drives away, blithely abandoning his novel to the reader who, like Nicholas, is first drawn into and then set free to resolve the godgame.

*The French Lieutenant's Woman* is, in one of its many aspects, Fowles's dramatization of his own theory of the novel. It is a metatheatrical work of literary criticism in which he examines not only the relationship between the novel genre's past, the traditional form, and the novel's potential in the future, but also the nature of the relationships that can exist between a novelist and his characters and between a novelist and his audience. Though he says in his essay on the composition of *The French Lieutenant's Woman* that the novel's traditional "purposes—to entertain, to satirize, to describe new sensibilities, to record life, to improve life, and so on—[are still] just as viable and important,"[7] he also envisions in *The French Lieutenant's Woman* how the living participation of the reader in the writing of the novel and in the lives of the novel's characters can lend much greater vitality to the novel as a living art form. Perhaps *The French Lieutenant's Woman* is most closely comparable to the freakishly popular rock musicals of the late sixties and early seventies—*Hair, Jesus Christ Superstar*, and *Godspell*—that owed their success to the participatory relationship they managed to create between the stage and the audience. When the playgoer or the novel reader

7. *Afterwords: Novelists on Their Novels*, 165.

actually participates in the work of art before him, then, in that moment, that particular art work comes alive for him and the strength of the life–art relationship is once more affirmed. If Fowles, as the novelist–god of *The French Lieutenant's Woman*, can draw his readers into participation in the very writing of his novel, then he can prove Conchis, who said that "fiction is the worst form of connection" (108), wrong.

Fowles the novelist–god first intrudes himself into the world of *The French Lieutenant's Woman* in Chapter thirteen. Here he defines his novel, which to this point had been a conventional historical novel, as a Pirandelloesque metanovel in which the characters who had momentarily found an author begin to rebel against that author's authority. He confesses that the

> characters I create never existed outside my own mind.
> If I have pretended until now to know my characters'
> minds and innermost thoughts, it is because I am writ-
> ing in . . . a convention usually accepted at the time
> of my story: that the novelist stands next to God. . . .
> But I live in the age of Alain Robbe-Grillet and Roland
> Barthes; if this is a novel, it cannot be a novel in the
> modern sense of the word. (80)

Not writing a *roman nouveau*, but nevertheless writing a novel in the best sense of the term, a novel that is simultaneously traditional and experimental, Fowles intrudes in Chapter thirteen in order to jolt the reader who, reading this seemingly traditional historical novel, is becoming too passively comfortable in his overstuffed armchair. He wants to start a dialogue with his reader as did Fielding who told his fellow stagecoach passengers the history of Tom Jones. But he also wants to make it clear that he is not a Fielding or a Thackeray, "a novelist [who] has only to pull the right strings and his puppets will behave in a lifelike manner; and produce a thorough analysis of their motives and intentions" (81). Clearly, almost in answer to Conchis, he is writing something more real than a historical novel. And so, in Chapter Thirteen of *The French Lieutenant's Woman*, Fowles attempts two kinds of liberation: First, he tries to free both himself and his characters from the tyrannizing roles of the traditional novelist–god/character relationship; and then, he attempts to free the reader from the traditional role of passive, uninvolved observer of the action that takes place in an unreal, fictional world.

The first liberation, of himself and of his characters, is easy for Fowles; he can accomplish it by simple proclamation. Ostensibly speaking for a collective group of "novelists," he explains to the startled reader why a traditional historical novel has suddenly metamorphosed into an animated lecture on literary theory:

> We know a world is an organism, not a machine. We also know that a genuinely created world must be independent of its creator; a planned world (a world that fully reveals its planning) is a dead world. It is only when our characters and events begin to disobey us that they begin to live. (81)
> In other words, to be free myself, I must give him, and Tina, and Sarah, even the abominable Mrs. Poulteney, their freedom as well. There is only one good definition of God: the freedom that allows other freedoms to exist. And I must conform to that definition. (82)

In theorizing this way about the freedom of his characters and the need for art to come alive, Fowles is informing the reader that the traditional novelist's god-game is being abandoned and that what follows will be an existential work of life–art.

Fowles becomes like the stage manager (he will

actually become an opera impresario near the end of the novel) in Pirandello's *Six Characters in Search of an Author*, unable to control the characters who have entered his previously traditional world and yet fascinated by the aura of reality that emanates from the free expression of their own lives. Fowles is saying also that if life and art do come together in *The French Lieutenant's Woman*, it happens, not because he has been able to construct a "reality," but because his characters do exist and demand of him that he justly portray the reality of their decisions and actions, the truth of their lives. In effect, *The French Lieutenant's Woman* is a committee novel, written by Fowles and Charles and Sarah and the others in collaboration, and near the end Fowles asks the reader to take his seat on the committee also.

Therefore, when Fowles in Chapter Thirteen, seemingly speaking with tongue in cheek, says, "Perhaps I am trying to pass off a concealed book of essays on you. Instead of chapter headings, perhaps I should have written . . . 'The History of the Novel Form'" (80–81), he is in fact introducing the abstract, aesthetic theme of his novel. He will not, however, present his "History of the Novel" in the form of a prose essay. Rather, his whole novel will be a metafictional dramatization of the past, the present, and the future of the novel genre. For the novelist–lecturer of Chapter Thirteen the

> novelist is still a god, since he creates (and not even the most aleatory avant-garde modern novel has managed to extirpate its author completely); what has changed is that we are no longer gods of the Victorian image, omniscient and decreeing; but in the new theological image, with freedom our first principle, not authority. (82)

Thus, Fowles liberates himself by means of a historical analysis both of the form in which he writes and of himself in writing in that form. And he liberates his characters by giving them the Sartrean prerogative of putting their existences before the essences that he as novelist–god might impose upon them.

The second liberation, that of the startled reader, will not, however, be as easy as the first. Naturally the reader is sceptical about the actual potential for the existence of "life" in an art form that everyone knows is, after all, "fictional." Fowles answers this scepticism by actually berating the reader, calling him a *"hypocrite lecteur,"* and by applying this theory of fictional art to the life of the reader and to the lives of all *"Homo sapiens"*:

> Fiction is woven into all. . . . I would have you share my own sense that I do not fully control these creatures of my mind, any more than you control . . . your children, colleagues, friends, or even yourself. . . . You do not even think of your own past as quite real: you dress it up, you gild it or blacken it, censor it, tinker with it . . . fictionalize it, in a word, and put it away on a shelf—your book, your romanced autobiography. We are all in flight from the real reality. (82)

Thus, fiction becomes the reality after all, and every man is an artist who writes the novel of his own life. If every man can liberate his central character, himself, as Fowles is liberating his characters, then each man can create art out of his own life.

Fowles ends *The French Lieutenant's Woman* conventionally in Chapter Forty-four. However, in accordance with his theory of art and life, Fowles explains in Chapter Forty-five that "having brought this fiction to a thoroughly traditional ending," the novel has not ended at all. Real novels, living art works, do not end appropriately and conveniently for both novelist and characters just as life does not always develop exactly the way it is supposed to. We are "all novelists," Fowles writes,

> that is, we have a habit of writing fictional futures for ourselves. . . . We screen in our minds hypotheses about how we might behave, about what might happen to us; and these novelistic . . . hypotheses often have very much more effect on how we actually do behave, when the real future becomes the present, than we generally allow. (266)

Novels and lives are like adulterous love affairs. Often, according to moral convention, such affairs are broken off because they should be. But more often than not they are resumed because the ending fails to satisfy the reality of the human emotions involved. Things stop and start up again every day in everyone's lives, and Fowles is simply making what is real in life real in his art.

In Chapter Forty-four Charles Smithson "felt himself coming to the end of a story; and to an end he did not like. . . . The book of his existence, so it seemed to him, was about to come to a distinctly shabby close" (266–67). To Charles, an omnipotent Victorian novelist is, for the sake of convention, imposing an essence upon his existence. But in Chapter Forty-five Charles takes on new life, and a different ending (or set of endings) begins. Just as Charles finds the conventional ending of a love affair with Sarah "distinctly shabby," so also does Fowles find the traditional Victorian ending to his novel unsatisfactory. Fowles's characters, like Pirandello's, refuse to be Victorianized (victimized, tyrannized), and the novel continues in order to fulfill itself as a lifelike work of art.

In order to accomplish this fulfillment of the life–

art relationship, Fowles actually becomes a character in his own novel. In his last two conversations with the still startled reader, he is no longer an intruding narrative voice, a lecturer. Rather, he becomes a physically described character, sitting, thinking, and walking, reflecting on the world of the novel. Just as his novel has a number of possible endings for the reader to choose from, so also does Fowles, when he becomes a character in his own novel, project two different aesthetic atittudes. When Fowles, as both novelist and character, enters Charles's first-class railway carriage in Exeter, he is a "prophet-bearded man" dressed as "a successful lay preacher" (316). "I stare at Charles," writes Fowles the novelist of Fowles the character, with "the look of an omnipotent god, [a] bizarre blend of the inquisitive and the magistral; of the ironic and the soliciting" (317).

But when Fowles the novelist–character appears again—loitering on the Chelsea embankment, glancing at Rossetti's house, winding his watch—he wears a different attitude:

> The once full, patriarchal beard of the railway compartment has been trimmed down to something rather foppish and Frenchified. . . . He looks very much as if he has given up preaching and gone in for grand opera. . . . He is staring back towards Mr. Rossetti's house; and with an almost proprietory air, as if it is some new theater he has just bought and is pretty confident he can fill . . . he very evidently regards the world as his to possess and use as he likes. (362)

From preacher to impresario, from omnipotent god to metatheatrical stage manager, Fowles the artist is undergoing the same kind of existential change that his central character, Charles Smithson, is experiencing. Fowles the novelist is learning about art what

Charles the character is learning about life: Real art and real life cannot be easily classified, cannot always be defined in terms of existent conventions. One of the novel's most definitive metaphors of the relationship of art to life is its portrayal of Victorian male chauvinism.

In *The French Lieutenant's Woman*, the central female character, Sarah Woodruff, has attained selfhood before the novel even begins. She knows who she is and in her own freedom she knows how to encourage the grasping of freedom by others. The antiexistential force in this novel is the conventional male. Charles nurtures an inbred attitude of possessiveness toward women; he at first refuses to recognize Sarah as capable of autonomous selfhood outside of any reference or relation to a man. To requote Camus's critical comment, "A novel is never anything but a philosophy expressed in images. And in a good novel the philosophy has disappeared into the images."[8] Fowles, in *The French Lieutenant's Woman*, has indeed immersed his existential philosophy of art in his male chauvinist theme.

Like the conventional male of the nineteenth and twentieth centuries, the novelist is plagued by possessiveness, of his characters' actions and of his readers' minds. The novelist finds it hard to give up possession of his characters, hard to let them act as self-conscious human beings outside of his jurisdiction. He finds it doubly difficult to allow his readers to direct the meaning of his work of art. As the "prophet-bearded man" in the railway carriage says,

> Fiction usually pretends to conform to the reality: the writer puts the conflicting wants in the ring and then describes the fight—but in fact fixes the fight, letting that want he himself favors win. And we judge writers of

8. *Lyrical and Critical Essays* (New York, 1968), 199.

fiction both by the skill they show in fixing the fights (in other words, in persuading us that they were not fixed) and by the kind of fighter they fix in favor of. (317)

When the "Frenchified" impresario appears in the last scene of the novel, his blithe aloofness indicates that he is no longer a fight fixer. Now, as an impresario, he is merely the sponsor of the entertainment, the promoter of the fight, rather than the "cannibalistic" preacher of "the bullying tabernacle kind" (316) who must possess his characters and direct his readers' responses. Fowles, with his conception of participatory fiction, succeeds in defeating in himself the aesthetic chauvinism that has ruled the novel genre since the Victorian Age. In *The French Lieutenant's Woman* Fowles defeats the "catatonia of convention" (300)— convention as a restriction upon human relationships, but more important, convention as a restriction upon art.

Thus, Fowles realizes that the twentieth-century novel cannot be content to accept the neatness of resolution of the conventional Victorian novel ending. That kind of acceptance rejects the often messy reality of the twentieth century, a century in which paradox is most often the only possible explanation of reality. Fowles's antidote for the "catatonia of convention" involves an existential experience for the reader. Fowles is like another innovative novelist from far back in the eighteenth century, Laurence Sterne in *Tristram Shandy*, who gave his reader a blank page on which to write a description of the Widow Wadman. Instead of a blank page, Fowles, in *The French Lieutenant's Woman*, gives his reader three potential endings from which to choose. J. Hillis Miller writes that the "words of a novel objectify the mind of an author and make that mind available to others."[9] This comment might well be applied to both Sterne and Fowles. Both, in their separate centuries, are attempting to dramatize their own ideas about how novels should be written, attempting to make their own minds available to their readers. Both attempts are fraught with the difficulty of bringing art and life together realistically; but, by means of metaphor and metatheater, art and life repeatedly complement each other in the metafiction of John Fowles.

Near the second-to-last ending of *The French Lieutenant's Woman* the following dialogue occurs between Sarah Woodruff and Charles Smithson and, metaphorically, between life and art:

> "I have since seen artists destroy work that might to the amateur seem perfectly good. I remonstrated once. I was told that if an artist is not his own sternest judge he is not fit to be an artist. I believe that is right. I believe I was right to destroy what had begun between us. . . ."
> "You . . . You cannot answer me with observations, however apposite, on art."
> "They were intended to apply to life as well."
> (351–52)

Each of Fowles's novels draws this same accord between life and art, and in what better place to give the art–life theme of his fiction its most explicit expression than in the studio of Rossetti, the Pre-Raphaelite painter and poet. As Rossetti, Ruskin, Pater, and Oscar Wilde all stressed, Fowles, in his characterizations, his descriptive style, the events of his novels, and in his own intruding voice, also emphasizes: Life and art must imitate each other.

9. *The Form of Victorian Fiction* (Notre Dame, Ind., 1968), 1.

# THE LONELINESS OF SELFHOOD

IN each of his novels, Fowles consistently displays his mastery of the art of objective correlation. Two basic themes complement each other in each novel: The aesthetic theme, which analyzes the relationship between art and life, is correlated to the existential theme, which dramatizes the struggles of individuals to define themselves and to make moral decisions about the conduct of their lives in worlds which discourage self-expression and deny existential freedom. Fowles's greatest strength as a novelist lies in his continuous and artful linking of these two themes. Ultimately, however, all meaning in fiction must acknowledge its dependence upon the literal— the plots, the images, the lives of intensely realized characters in a physical world.

Fowles himself, writing about *The French Lieutenant's Woman*, focuses upon the primary importance of the human plots and images of his novels:

> The Victorian Age, especially from 1850 on, was highly existentialist in many of its personal dilemmas. One can almost invert the reality and say that Camus and Satre have been trying to lead us, in their fashion, to a Victorian seriousness of purpose and moral sensitivity.[1]

Fowles embodies his philosophical and aesthetic themes in the "personal dilemmas" of his characters and in the imagistic representation of the world and society in which those characters must define their existences. Because existentialism is concerned solely with individual lives in the physical world, those lives and that world must be brought to life before any

1. *Afterwords: Novelists on Their Novels*, 165–66.

philosophical lesson can be embodied in action. And Fowles, like the great Victorian preexistential novelists —Dickens, Eliot, Hardy, Conrad—creates an intensely realized world by means of detailed physical description. He accomplishes his characterizations by means of dramatized scenes in which real people enact their destinies and display their humanity, or lack of it.

In each of Fowles's novels, for example, the theme of isolation is represented both in the human situations and in the images. Fowles's central characters—Miranda, Nicholas, Charles, and Sarah—are all questers for themselves, searchers trying to find their own existences. Ultimately, all experience the loneliness of selfhood. That loneliness is like the experience of shipwreck or, as in *The Collector*, of kidnap. Suddenly, irrationally, a person is torn from a safe, insulated, static life among his own kind and cast ashore on or thrust into an undefined world where the rules of life are different (or are nonexistent); and he becomes an isolated alien who must define himself in order to survive. As Fowles writes in *The Aristos*, "We are all Crusoes; no one knows our happiness, and unhappiness, like ourselves" (63).

In *The Aristos* Fowles confronts the fact of midtwentieth-century isolation and the recurring situation of the loneliness of selfhood by means of both statement and image:

> Our stereotyping societies force us to feel more alone. They stamp masks on us and isolate our real selves. . . . The more society interferes and supervises and plays the good Samaritan, the less needed and lonelier the secret individual gets. . . . The more science reveals our mechanical nature the more a harried "free" man, a Robin Hood in each, retreats into the forests of the private mind. . . . Yet all those lonelinesses are a part of our growing up, of our first going out alone, of our

freedom. A child is protected from such fear and loneliness by having a falsely kind and simple mirage erected around him. He grows up and goes out into loneliness and reality and there he builds a more real protection against his isolation out of love and friendship and feeling for his fellow men. (39–40)

Not only does Fowles state the fact of modern man's isolation and loneliness here but, despite his protestations at the beginning of *The Aristos* that he would shun "all persuasion through style" (13), he represents this loneliness in a series of images. In *The Aristos* (and in each of the novels) the concepts of isolation and the loneliness of selfhood are presented by means of spatial images. Man becomes a "Robin Hood" retreating into the enclosure of the "forests of the private mind." Loneliness is man's "first going out alone," a transition from protected space to the hostile open space of the real world. A child is initially enclosed in love, a "mirage erected around him," but must eventually "go out into loneliness" and build a "more real protection against his isolation."

For Fowles the existential journey to selfhood is a traveling out of the enclosures of isolation, a passage through the thick walls of loneliness. The quester traverses a landscape of inner and outer spaces that symbolically oppose each other. In Fowles's novels the protagonists invariably are trapped in claustrophobic rooms, often underground, and left in isolation to discover themselves. Just as they are physically forced inside, so also are they mentally forced to look within to contemplate the depths of their own psyches. The Fowles landscape, however, also includes the other spatial pole in which the lessons learned, the selfhood found in the isolation of inner space, can be exercised in an outdoor world of human relationships. The

Fowles world is balanced between indoor scenes of isolation and occasional violence; and freer, healthier outdoor scenes of people trying to reach out, communicate, and love each other. Isolation is necessary for selfhood and for humanization, and thus Fowles states, spatially images, and dramatizes isolation as the major existential theme of his fiction. Fowles's protagonists may emerge from the underground and find themselves still isolated, but at least this outer isolation is freely chosen and not imposed by an insane world or caused by the protagonists' own lack of selfhood.

The most frequently recurrent spatial images in Fowles's fiction are the motifs of closed, underground rooms (embodying the concept of imprisonment) and explicitly bounded settings (representing the restrictions that society can impose upon the life of the un-self-conscious individual). Even in *The Aristos*, that supposedly "unstyled" work, spatial motifs appear. For example, Fowles describes individual lives as

> the houses we live in. They may not be the most desirable houses we can imagine, we may wish they were larger, more beautiful, newer, older—but we accept that this is the house we have to live in now, and we do our best to make it habitable. I am not a temporary tenant, a casual lodger in my present life. (36)

But even though one recognizes the value of his own house of life, the anxieties of living in the modern world are still a constant threat that must be faced by everyone. "These anxieties should make us one. We all feel them. But we let them isolate us, as if the citizens of a country would defend it by each barricading himself in his own house" (42). When a human being enters into this kind of isolation, then the house of life becomes a prison.

Life as a prison is the spatial concept upon which

the other major imagistic motif of *The Aristos* is based. Fowles's main point about the prison of life, however, is not that man must escape from it but that he must learn to exist within it. Echoing his predecessors in the existential prison novel—Stendhal, Dostoevsky, Camus, Malamud—Fowles acknowledges that life is "a prison cell, but it is, or can be made to become, a comparatively spacious one; and inside it we can become relatively free" (68). For a wife marriage can become "the domestic prison, those grim four walls constituted by husband, children, housework and kitchen" (172), or for an artist life within society can give a "sense of imprisonment in the mass of other artists. Prison destroys personal identity; and this is what the artist now most fears" (193). Thus, too often, the idea of imprisonment seems to be a threat to personal identity; but, as Julien Sorel, Raskolnikov, Meursault, and the Fixer discover, this is not always the case. Men in the modern world, Fowles writes in his "unstyled" *The Aristos*, "are like prisoners vainly and laboriously trying to file their way through massive iron bars in order to reach a blue sky in which they could not possibly exist; while all the time, just behind them, their cell waits to be properly lived in" (213). In *The Aristos*, Fowles somewhat sketchily images man's need to confront the anxieties of existence in both inner and outer space. Man must confront the claustrophobic reality of his own inner self as well as the poisonous atmosphere of the social world. Fowles presents this same world view much more fully and meaningfully in the spatial imagistic motifs of his novels.

Where for the psychological novelist such as D. H. Lawrence phallic and womb symbols describe different aspects of a character's subconscious personality, for the existential novelist spatial images become objective correlatives for the relationship between the individual self and the world in which that self can either exist, or conflict, or be lost. Setting becomes overtly symbolic because the existential writer is most concerned with man's relationship to the world and the way the world controls or influences life. Fowles, perhaps owing to his admiration of the fiction of Thomas Hardy, is always aware, as Hardy the architect–novelist was, of the potentially symbolic uses of distinctive settings. Tess's isolation from the world as she sleeps on Stonehenge's pagan altar is comparable to the isolation of Sarah Woodruff when Charles Smithson sees her asleep in the sun on a ledge in the Undercliff. The many other symbolic scenes that occur in Fowles's Undercliff also summon associations similar to those which have so often been made about George Eliot's symbolic use of the Red Deeps in *The Mill on the Floss*. In *The Magus* Fowles shipwrecks his central character, Nicholas, on a symbolic island of the self. During his stay on that island Nicholas must explore every part of it, descend beneath its surface placidity to learn its secrets. He must define the real existential life of the drowsy, seemingly unconcerned island of the modern self. It is *The Collector*, however, that displays Fowles's most obvious use of spatial imagery and symbolic setting.

When Clegg first sees the underground cellar in which he will later keep Miranda, he is stunned: "It was like down there didn't exist. It was two worlds" (19). With the flashing of this thought across Clegg's mind, the imagery of the opposition between inner and outer space in *The Collector* begins. Clegg later thrusts Miranda into this underground room, thus forcing her to confront the less accessible of the "two worlds" of the novel, the world of her inner self.

By isolating his existentially unformed (that is, not yet self-conscious) heroine in an underground room, Fowles creates a situation in which two of his basic ideas about human nature can be symbolized in action. First, Miranda's introspection in the isolation of the underground room symbolizes the need of men for introspection into their own personalities. When she is thrust into the room, Miranda is also forced to look into herself and for the first time to ask the questions: Who am I? What does my life mean? What can I contribute to the world outside of this newly explored room of my own selfhood? The repeated imaging of the opposition between the closed, inner world of the room and the open, outer world makes Fowles's second point: Man must withdraw into inner space in order to define himself.

The knowledge gained in the lonely exploration of private inner space, however, is of no value if it cannot be put to use in the outer world. The secrets of inner space, however, the knowledge of the real self, must be freed from the underground prisons that are maintained by social convention, personal hypocrisy, and the antiexistential fear of self-expression and involvement. The liberation of the self can only be accomplished by means of moral, human action in the outer world. Miranda grows despite the meager supplies of light and air in her inner space, but she is frustrated in her attempts to take the second step into full selfhood. She cannot accomplish the liberation of her inner self, and therein lies the tragedy of *The Collector*.

At different times in *The Collector* the underground room is described as a "lunatic asylum" (102) and a "crypt" (122), but most often it is a secure prison, much more real than the metaphorical prisons of

*The Aristos.* Clegg, employing Gestapo tactics learned from books, will not allow Miranda any newspapers because he has read "how one of the first things to put up with if you were a prisoner was the not knowing what was going on outside the prison" (40). Miranda sees the underground room as a "luxury prison" (213), but she wants desperately to escape, just as the netted butterfly tries vainly to fly away. In fact, the butterfly motif and the prison motif in *The Collector* correlate closely in their symbolic representation of the potential alternatives for the existential self. The victim of society's insane repression of the self can either die in prison or, having found identity in prison, be set free to express that newfound selfhood by means of social involvement in the outer world. In the same way, the butterfly image is symbolic of rebirth out of inner space. Miranda is the caterpillar who enters the cocoon to emerge later into a new, mature self. Unfortunately, the collector, who with curiosity has been observing her growth in the cocoon, decides to become the passive killer who destroys life by standing by and doing nothing. Miranda, as she emerges from the cocoon with a new identity, drops right into Clegg's killing bottle. Like Julien Sorel and Camus's Meursault, at the moment Miranda finds existential life by going within herself she must face physical death by decree of the outer world.

The vast difference between the underground world of *The Collector*, where Miranda gains valuable knowledge about her self, and the outer world of freedom is vividly imaged in the symbolic definition of setting. When Clegg allows Miranda outside she revels in

> great reaches of clear sky, no moon, sprinkles of warm white stars everywhere, like milky diamonds, and a

> beautiful wind. . . . The branches rustling, an owl hoot-
> ing in the woods. And the sky all wild, all free, all
> wind and air and space and stars. . . .
>   Indoors it couldn't have been more different. (169)

The outer world in all of its variety and beauty symbolizes life and the expansiveness of self-expression.
But in the inner space of her underground prison, Miranda's self-in-isolation must exist in "'strange dead
air" (120). Momentarily freed from her cell, in the
lounge of the house after a walk outdoors, Miranda defines the spatial symbolism in terms of an air image.
"That air was wonderful," she exclaims. "Even this
air. It's free. It's everything I'm not" (50). The self can
be found in the isolation of the underground, but it has
to return to the world of fresh air and light before it
can really come to life.

     As a submotif, the light imagery of *The Collector*
complements the different uses of spatial imagery.
Light imagery is especially appropriate because as an
artist Miranda is acutely aware of the shortcomings of
artificial light. Thus, Miranda can deem her first escape attempt a success, though she reaches only the
outer cellar, because she catches a glimpse of a "key-
holeful of light" (118). "The thing I miss most is
fresh light," she admits in an epistolary paragraph to
her sister Minny, "I can't live without light. Artificial
light, all the lines lie" (117). Just as a keyhole is a
small tunnel between a closed room and an open world,
so are the changing images of air (fresh or dead) and
light (natural, artificial, or absent) passages between
the two different and symbolically opposed spatial
worlds of the novel. Alone in the darkness, Miranda
can only look within herself. She tries repeatedly, first
in her escape attempts and then in her attempts to
establish a relationship with Clegg, to traverse the

tunnel to the wider world. Each time, however, Clegg rolls a huge stone across the mouth of the tunnel (screws tight the unperforated top of the killing bottle) shutting off access to air and to light. Fowles's spatial consciousness in *The Collector* symbolically defines the existential quest of Miranda for her own selfhood. Forced to turn inward, she finds her real self, but when she tries to express that new self to the outer world, no one listens. She dies, trapped in the loneliness of selfhood.

In *The Magus* Fowles again creates a spatially symbolic setting. His central character, Nicholas Urfe, chooses to pursue the existential quest on an explicitly bounded island of the self. Quite early in the novel Nicholas facetiously quotes John Donne's line, "No man is an island," to Conchis who quite seriously replies:

> Pah. Rubbish. Every one of us is an island. If it were not so we should go mad at once. Between these islands are ships, airplanes, telephones, television—what you will. But they remain islands. Islands that can sink or disappear forever. You are an island that has not sunk. (141)

The island of Phraxos is a symbol of Nicholas's interior space, which must be defined and understood before he can ever go outside himself and establish a truly human relationship with another person. Nicholas's very first introduction to Conchis is an invitation to explore this interior space. On a secluded beach in a book of poetry planted by Conchis, Nicholas finds, especially marked for him, these lines from T. S. Eliot's "Little Gidding":

> *We shall not cease from exploration*
> *And the end of all our exploring*

> *Will be to arrive where we started*
> *And know the place for the first time.* (65)

Exploring the island is a spatial metaphor for exploring the self. Once Nicholas can understand the secrets
of Bourani (which means "skull") and appreciate the
motives of Conchis (pronounced with a soft "ch"), then
his own new consciousness will qualify him to return
to the world of human relationships, first with Jojo and
finally with Alison.

Nicholas begins exploring the island as his only
means of escaping the "claustrophobic ambience of the
Lord Byron School" (47). But soon, Rousseau-like,
Nicholas perceives that the island is "as potential as a
clean canvas, a site for myths" (59). His whole existence on this island of the self is a *tabula rasa* that
must be written upon and given definition. Crusoe-
like, he feels a "metaphysical sense of being ma-
rooned" (54), the "total enislement from all else"
(226), the "sense of existential solitude, the being and
being alone in a universe" (335). Like Miranda closed
up in an airless underground room, Nicholas on Phraxos perceives the loneliness of selfhood.

But this motif, the exploration of the island of
interior space, is only one of the spatial motifs of *The
Magus*. As in *The Collector*, the imagery of closed
rooms as opposed to the natural, outdoor world of
crisp air and brilliant sunlight is very evident. Early
in the novel Alison and Nicholas make love in closed
rooms. Despite their physical union, they are isolated
from each other because Nicholas is unable to love and
able only to deceive, both Alison and himself. Later
however, after Nicholas has experienced loneliness,
they make love in the open, natural, sun-drenched
outer space of Mount Parnassus. Though this spontaneous union is only a momentary conquering of both

Nicholas's and Alison's isolation—immediately upon descending the mountain Alison, cursing Nicholas, locks herself in a closed Athens hotel room—it does illustrate a theme present in every Fowles novel: Real life exists only in those "moments when the otherness of the other" (50) is defeated. In the Russell Square apartment Nicholas and Alison breathe air "full of unspoken words, unformulated guilts, a vicious silence, like the moments before a bridge collapses" and they lie "side by side, untouching, effigies on a bed turned tomb" (35). Parnassus, however, is "a world both literally and metaphorically of light" (245) where "the sunlight on the glade, the white roar of the little fall, the iciness, the solitude, the laughing, the nakedness [creates] moments one knows only death can obliterate," where Alison becomes "a poem" that denies all "the unpoetic accretions of modern life" (225).

The spatial imagery of *The Magus* takes still another form in the metaphor of "the waiting room," which defines Nicholas's existential situation during his education at Bourani. As a reprieved prisoner waits in the anteroom of the penitentiary to be released, Nicholas in his year on Phraxos also marks time between the worlds of death and renewed life. The "beware the waiting room" warning is life-denying, and luckily Nicholas ignores it. In another sense, the waiting room is where a man waits to see his doctor in hopes of being cured of a disease. When Nicholas first enters the waiting room, having only recently subdued his suicidal impulses, he is suffering from lack of selfhood, a common deficiency in self-deceiving men. Conchis, the doctor, will prescribe participation in the godgame as a potential cure. The "SALLE D'ATTENTE" (67) is also where a man waits before embarking on a journey. When he first enters the "domaine,"

Nicholas is waiting to descend into his heart of darkness, as was Marlow who sat in the Brussels waiting room of the trading company. Near the end of *The Magus*, as Nicholas waits in London for Alison to reappear, he realizes that "freedom was making some abrupt choice and acting on it" and he longs "to break out of this waiting room" where he has been detaining himself. Enclosure in the waiting room is the first step on the mythic journey into interior space; and bursting out, like a diver from the depths, into air, light, and human involvement is the last step on the journey to selfhood.

The combination of spatial imagery with the myth of the descent into the underground that first appeared in *The Collector* is also renewed in the underground rooms of *The Magus*. The first symbolic descent into the underground, however, is Conchis's, and it occurs in the form of a narrated flashback to World War I. Conchis tells of awakening from the "long sleep" (118) of unself-conscious life when the shells begin to explode around him and the battle of Neuve-Chapelle begins. For Conchis, entering the battle is a descent into the underworld of death: "If there is a hell, then it is that" (118), he tells Nicholas. On the second day of Conchis's battle in retrospect, he descends even further into the underground of a shell hole which he shares for two days and nights with the half-decayed, half-eaten corpse of a German soldier and with a pack of feasting rats. Conchis tells the story because, in accord with the archetype, this descent into the underground is a turning point in his life. In the shell crater he experiences the loneliness of selfhood, but that loneliness is mere inconvenience when compared to the utter nothingness of the death raining down all around him. He learns that being existentially alive even though alone is better than having no selfhood at all.

Nicholas also must descend, twice, into the underground where all the deceptive romance of life is destroyed and only the loneliness of selfhood remains to be either embraced or rejected. Nicholas first enters the symbolic underground when he descends with Julie into the "unpleasantly claustrophobic" (415) underground room, a converted World War II German gun emplacement, used by Conchis's repertory meta-theater group as dormitory, prop room, and makeup salon. As Julie and Nicholas prepare to leave this restricted inner space of "the earth" (416), he longs for the romantic, idyllic openness of outer space:

> a place under the bluff on the central ridge, a little corner shaded by pine trees, absolutely private, thickly carpeted with pine needles; to take her there, to take her, with a gentle roughness, a romantic brutality; as, and I did not shirk the parallel, I had taken Alison on Parnassus. (416)

Immediately this romantic projection into human involvement in outer space is shattered as Conchis's henchmen tear Julie away and slam the lid, leaving Nicholas alone in the underworld of inner space.

Nicholas escapes from "the earth" but soon, like Miranda in *The Collector*, he is drugged, kidnapped, and thrust into another underground room where he will undergo his disintoxication. Alone, Nicholas thinks upon Lily's betrayal of him to the kidnappers, and then his thoughts turn to the dead Alison. Could Alison's death be a betrayal too? "Then my mind plunged sickeningly," he writes, "as if I had walked off the edge of the world. . . . I let my mind wander into a bottomless madness" (440). The spatial images that Nicholas uses in his description—plunging into abysses of nothingness, wandering into bottomless psychological pits—define his entrance into his own interior space, his descent into his own heart of darkness. In this underground world he is first judged by the living Tarot deck that metamorphoses into an international panel of Freudian psychoanalysts; then he is disintoxicated from Lily by means of the juxtaposition of the pornographic movie and the living *Maja Desnuda.*

As he moves from one underground room to another, all of his romantic deceptions about himself and about his relationship with Lily are raped and slashed, mercilessly exposed in the harsh light of reality. Forced to descend into inner space, Nicholas sees his own mind, his motives, and himself for the first time. He emerges from this underworld a new man; phoenix-like, all of his self-deceptions have been burned away, and as Odysseus emerged from the land of the dead, Nicholas longs to apply his newfound self-knowledge by returning to the real world that he had left so long before.

Charles Smithson in *The French Lieutenant's Woman* also confronts himself and evaluates his own life in a mythic underground of interior space. Late in the novel, in the small, squalid room of a London prostitute, as he dangles his watch before her gurgling child, Charles realizes, in the spatial imagery of his own immediate situation, the truth necessary for survival in the "strange, dark labyrinths of life." He comes to the

> profound and genuine intuition of the great human illusion about time, which is that its reality is like that of a road—on which one can constantly see where one was and where one probably will be—instead of the

truth: that time is a room, a now so close to us that we regularly fail to see it. (252)

The picturing of life as a closed room that man must furnish and then open to the outside world is present in each Fowles novel. But this passage from *The French Lieutenant's Woman* combines the idea of time with that spatial imagery. Existential man can live only in present time; therefore each individual situation in a man's life, each meeting with another person (wanderer in the labyrinth), each moment of isolated introspection, is another room to be explored, lived in, and opened up to others.

While time and life are imaged as an underground room of present existence in *The French Lieutenant's Woman*, the image of the boundaried island of the self is also repeated as another objective correlative for the themes of isolation and introspection. The metaphor of man as an island is taken this time not from Donne but from Matthew Arnold's "To Marguerite." The metaphor of the island, on the surface isolated from the other islands of the world but below the surface, in the real self, connected to the rest of the world, defines again the theme of individual man's need for self-exploration followed by self-expression in the outer world of others. Charles Smithson is described as a man set adrift in his age, experiencing shipwreck in the "dangerous waters" (134, 153) of existential self-realization. As Charles faces the reality of Sarah (and simultaneously realizes his own lack of selfhood), he feels himself caught in "a maze of crosscurrents . . . swept hopelessly away from his safe anchorage" (143) into "dark depths" (197), into "eyes a man could drown in" (180). Sarah's entry into Charles's life shatters that life, turns his existence in a new direction as if "his ship had struck a reef" (359).

In *The French Lieutenant's Woman*, however, one of the most meaningful imagistic expressions of the theme of existential isolation is accomplished by means of a variation on the spatial images of the underground room that appeared in both *The Collector* and *The Magus*. The recurrent metaphor of the tunnel in *The French Lieutenant's Woman* supports the theme of the interior journey toward the self. Unlike the underground room of *The Collector*, which had no opening to the outside world, not even the small tunnel of a keyhole, the image of the tunnel in *The French Lieutenant's Woman* represents not only isolation and introspection in inner space but also movement through inner space to an existential destination in the world of light at the end of the tunnel. Fowles dramatizes the interior journey of Charles Smithson in a succession of confrontation scenes set in the symbolic landscape of the Undercliff. Sarah, Charles's Dantesque guide, leads him on his successive journeys into the mythic underground of the Undercliff, draws him ever forward and deeper into the tunnel of himself.

In their first meeting in the Undercliff, Sarah and Charles do not communicate at all. He comes upon her as she reclines in sunlit sleep on a secluded ledge. When they meet inadvertently a second time, they talk briefly, and Charles begins to feel the attraction of Sarah. Their third meeting in the Undercliff is much less inadvertent. As he searches for fossilized "tests" that he now automatically associates with "women lying asleep on sunlit ledges" (111), Charles pushes through "a kind of tunnel" of foliage at the end of which lies a clearing "bounded on all sides by dense bramble thickets" (112). Exploring this womblike tunnel, Charles suddenly finds Sarah staring at him from above "where the tunnel of ivy ended" (113).

Dramatically, "an oblique shaft of wan sunlight" pierces into the tunnel and illuminates Sarah's

> figure standing before the entombing greenery behind her; and her face was suddenly very beautiful, truly beautiful, exquisitely grave and yet full of an inner, as well as outer, light. (113)

Thus begins a scene of symbolic sexual comedy that unfolds at Charles's expense. Sarah hands Charles two "tests," symbols of his fossilized manhood. He tries to escape the confrontation—he stands "by the ivy, as if at a door" (115) and parts "the wall of ivy with his stick" (114)—but he cannot move. He cannot pull out of the womblike tunnel, yet he is afraid to thrust himself into a relationship with the mysterious Sarah. Comically, Charles becomes a frightened virgin, taking on "the role of Alarmed Propriety" (118), and the confrontation scene ends with Charles "breaking through the further curtain of ivy and stumbling on his downhill way, a good deal more like a startled roebuck than a worldly English gentleman" (119). Fowles's combining of womb symbolism with the imagery of the tunnel defines the overtly sexual relationship with Sarah that Charles must accept before he can progress any further on the interior journey into the tunnel of the self. In this scene Charles comes to the mouth of the tunnel and looks in, but like a teenage boy exploring his willing girlfriend for the first time, he is afraid to enter. He does, however, realize later how affected, timid, hypocritical, and utterly conventional his attitudes are, and when he next meets Sarah in the Undercliff, he determines to follow her into the tunnel of the self.

When Charles returns to the Undercliff a few days later, Sarah is waiting for him "in the shadows at the tunnel of ivy's other end" (133). The aura of sinister sexuality still radiates from Sarah, and Charles, the "startled roebuck" of the earlier scene, is still encased in his self- and truth-denying Victorian conventionality, anxious "to establish a distance, to remind her of their difference of station" (134). She leads him further through "another green tunnel" into a "dell, surrounded by thickets of brambles and dogwood . . . in all ways protected" (135). Journeying into the tunnel of the self, Charles penetrates to this womblike dell where Sarah opens herself to him, confesses her sexual "sin." The definition of this scene as an interior journey through a spatially and sexually symbolic landscape is made evident in the comments of the omniscient narrator, who says of Charles, "Deep in himself he forgave her her unchastity; and glimpsed the dark shadows where he might have enjoyed it himself." Expanding out of this one human relationship the narrator goes on to define the human isolation of the whole Victorian Age, again in terms of spatial and sexual imagery:

> There was that strangely Egyptian quality among the Victorians; that claustrophilia we see so clearly evidenced in their enveloping, mummifying clothes, their narrow-windowed and -corridored architecture, their fear of the open and of the naked. Hide reality, shut out nature. . . . Thus to Charles the openness of Sarah's confession—both so open in itself and in the open sunlight—seemed less to present a sharper reality than to offer a glimpse of an ideal world. (143)

This spatial imagery has its mythic dimension also. In these scenes in the Undercliff, the image of Sarah fixes in Charles's mind "an idea of what a siren looked like." She becomes "a Calypso" who is comically "matched by an Odysseus with a face acceptable in the best clubs" (117). Like Odysseus, who lives

96

tamely captivated in Calypso's cavern, who escapes from the underground cave of Polyphemus, and who descends into the world of the dead where he finds himself and learns the value of life, Charles Smithson makes a number of descents into the sexual underground of London where he learns, from a prostitute named Sarah, a lesson about love among the ruins of life. Finally, he makes the decisive descent, in two steps, into the shady, no-questions-asked world of Exeter.

His first step takes him into the maze of Endicott's Family Hotel where he finds Sarah, abandons all of his Victorian sexual conventionality and, no longer a "startled roebuck," enters into a relationship with her. After they make love, Charles rests "in the sweetest possession of his life, the last man alive, infinitely isolated" (275). He has, or so he thinks, followed the tunnel all the way to its end.

After leaving Sarah, Charles takes his second step. He "plunged, without realizing it, into that morally dark quarter of Exeter" (280). There he enters an unlighted, empty church where he undergoes a dark night of the soul. Standing on the edge of a "bottomless brink" (285), as he had stood earlier in the evening with his hand poised ready to knock on Sarah's door, Charles undergoes, as the Victorian Age itself eventually would, a conversion away from conventional belief and organized church morality into a more humanistic religious context such as Hardy imagined in *Jude the Obscure*. Charles emerges from this dark, empty, inner space a different, freer man, "shriven of established religion" (288) forever. The mythic night journey negotiated, Charles, like Odysseus, must put his newfound self-knowledge to work in the daylight world.

Thus, in each Fowles novel the existential journey into self finds objective correlation in spatial imagery. However, one other recurringly evident motif also represents this journey into self. Fowles's central characters—Miranda, Nicholas, Charles Smithson—are always looking in mirrors, as if trying to penetrate their own self-deceits by looking themselves in the eye. In the Fowles world, when a character looks at herself or himself in the mirror, the seen image forces self-analysis.

Self-realization in the Fowles world becomes a process of projection of the image of the external self outward (into a mirror or into a godgame or into a love affair with a mysterious woman), and then the truth-telling reflection of that superficial image backward upon the real self that the character has never known or has always avoided.

In *The Collector* Miranda experiences this very projection/reflection process as she learns to live with her loneliness and isolation:

> Something I have been doing a lot these last days. Staring at myself in the mirror. Sometimes I don't seem real to myself, it suddenly seems that it isn't my reflection only a foot or two away. I have to look aside. I look all over my face, at my eyes, I try to see what my eyes say. What I am. Why I'm here.
>
> It's because I'm so lonely. I have to look at an intelligent face. Anyone who has been locked away like this would understand. You become very real to yourself in a strange way. As you never were before. (206–7)

In the loneliness of her imprisonment, Miranda cannot "look aside" from herself. For the first time she looks within and finds her "real" self, the genuine Miranda who had been so illusive in her butterfly flights with Piers and G.P. in her unself-conscious, preunderground world. If only she could escape to that outer space taking this newfound self-knowledge with her; but, in *The Collector*, the mirror shatters hopelessly.

The patterning and the meaning of the mirror imagery in *The Magus* is, as is the novel itself, much more complex than in *The Collector*. In the fantastic, carnival world of Bourani, Conchis is a jaded and ironic magician, who might well say to Nicholas, the wide-eyed rube who has just asked how that finale trick was performed, "It's all done with mirrors." "I went and washed, stared at myself in the mirror," Nicholas writes about the morning after his psychic trip under the mesmeric power of Conchis, whom he calls "Svengali" (227). One doesn't stare into a mirror unless one is explicitly looking for something, some change, or some feature never seen before.

Later, betrayed by Lily, captured and being transported by ship to his disintoxication in the underground, Nicholas looks at the mural painted on the wall of his shipboard cabin:

> It was a huge black figure, larger than lifesize, a kind
> of living skeleton, a Buchenwald figure, lying on its
> side on what might have been grass, or flames. A gaunt
> hand pointed down to a little mirror hanging on the
> wall; exhorting me, I suppose, to look at myself. . . .
> I went and looked in the *memento mori* mirror. . . .
> Alison. I stared at my own dilated eyes in the mirror.
> Suddenly her honesty, her untreachery—her death—
> was the last anchor left. If she, if she . . . I was swept
> away. The whole of life became a conspiracy.(439–40)

In this mirror confrontation Nicholas begins to realize the difference between the illusion and the reality of himself. He expresses his hope that Alison is not one of the magician's many mirror illusions. He depends upon the fact of Alison's reality—"she was a mirror that did not lie; whose interest in me was real; whose love was real. That had been her supreme virtue: a constant reality" (487)—and when that mirror also proves to be illusory, he is thrown back upon the only possible reality, the self in isolation. In the loneliness of selfhood he rejects the false mirror images that have flashed at him from every side during his progress through Conchis's godgame, and he honestly accepts himself for the first time.

The world and the people of *The Magus* are defined as mirrors into which Nicholas must look in order to find his real self. The scenes of the meta-theatrical godgame that are so meticulously choreographed by Conchis are all distorting mirrors. The whole intent of the godgame is for Nicholas to look closely into these mirrors and there to discover his own distorted image. "Greece is like a mirror," Conchis tells Nicholas, "It makes you suffer. Then you learn. . . . To live. With things as they are" (95). That telling question which De Deukans had asked Conchis and which Conchis in turn poses to Nicholas—"Which are you drinking? The water or the wave? "—is a question that "should always be asked. It is not a precept. But a mirror" (183). Like Alison, Lily also is a mirror that shatters into different and ambiguous images. At one moment she is the Victorian Lily; at the next she is the mid-twentieth-century Julie; at another time she is the Freudian Dr. Maxwell or the fleeing Artemis–Diana or the naked *maja*. Nicholas can never capture the illusion that is Lily, yet in contemplating her changing image he is able to find himself: "Narcissus-like I saw my own face reflected deep in her indecision, her restlessness" (269).

But Lily is only one part of the complex maze of mirrors in which Nicholas wanders. The hall of mirrors is the godgame and Nicholas has been given a ticket of entry by Conchis, the magician who runs the funhouse. Nicholas enters the hall of mirrors a wide-eyed rube mindlessly laughing at his own grotesquely shifting image as it moves across the glass walls. But the novelty of distortion, the comicality of grotesqueness, wears off quickly, and soon turns into simple ugliness and pathetic deformity. Before Nicholas even enters the hall of mirrors, Conchis describes, by alluding to his own past experience, what lies within:

> Something had been waiting there all my life. I stood there, and I knew who waited, who expected. It was myself. I was here and this house was here, and they had always been here, like reflections of my own coming. It was like a dream. I had been walking towards a closed door, and by a sudden magic its impenetrable wood became glass, through which I saw myself coming from the other direction, the future. (104–5)

When Nicholas breaks out of the hall of mirrors, the godgame, he is a different man from the one who could laugh at the distorted reflections of himself. He can exist no longer in self-distortion and he longs for the self that is natural and genuine.

In *The French Lieutenant's Woman* Charles Smithson tries to "interrogate his good-looking face in the mirror" (27). Unlike Nicholas Urfe who is bombarded with grotesque images that mirror the distortions of his own selfhood, Charles Smithson repeatedly stares at a clear image of himself in the mirror and asks that image questions. Early in the novel, he carries on puzzled and insecure dialogues with himself via the mirror. Playfully, he can make faces at himself, "put a decade on his face: all gravity, the solemn young paterfamilias" or indulge in "affectionate contemplation of his features," but eventually he begins seeing reality in the mirror image: "Upon examination, it was a faintly foolish face. . . . Too innocent a face, when it was stripped of its formal outdoor mask." At this early stage of what will be a continuing and intense process of self-examination, Charles avoids the shallowness reflected in his shaving mirror. He proceeds "to cover the ambiguous face in lather" (38), unable yet to confront the fact of his own superficiality.

Later in the novel, however, he can no longer deny himself by simply smothering his face in lather. He sees that his mirror image is just as one-dimensional as he is, a smooth, superficial reflection of the conventionality, class prejudice, and affectation of the Victorian Age: So easily can a man become an image. His predicament is like that of the politician in the age of McLuhan who, at the urging of his imagemakers, compromises his principles in order to be elected and then realizes that he cannot ever regain his original moral credibility.

After this initial realization about men and their images, Charles begins to feel more comfortable with himself:

> He still felt, as he had told Sarah, a stranger to himself; but now it was with a kind of awed pleasure that he stared at his face in the mirror. He felt a great courage in himself, both present and future—and a uniqueness, a having done something unparalleled. And he had his wish: he was off on a journey again, a journey made doubly delicious by its promised companion. (291)

Having committed himself to Sarah, Charles can finally look himself in the eye, and he is ready to begin the journey through the looking glass into the inner self. In Charles Smithson's case that self has been so long repressed by the "catatonia of convention" (300) that he is indeed a stranger, a Victorian version of Camus's *l'etranger*, Meursault, on the beach after killing the Arab. Having committed a major Victorian crime, a sexual sin, Charles stands on the threshold of the journey into the inner self. Whereas Meursault's journey is into the spatially symbolic isolation of the prison, Charles's journey is into the abstract loneliness of selfhood. Unfortunately, and ironically, he must embark without his "promised" companion, Sarah, who disappears into the depths of London.

But whether alone or with Sarah, Charles's most significant revelation is that the journey into self must be undertaken. When he catches "sight of himself in a mirror" he sees that "the man in the mirror, Charles in another world, seemed the true self" and the smug English gentleman outside the mirror had always been simply "an imposter, an observed other" (299). Like Conchis and Nicholas in the magic hall of mirrors of Bourani, Charles Smithson sees his potential future self, an existential self undistorted by social conventions or hypocritical masks, coming toward him in the mirror. And he, like Nicholas, journeys to meet that beckoning "true self."

By means of spatially symbolic settings and existential image patterns, such as the motif of the mirror, the theme of the loneliness of selfhood is repeatedly symbolized in Fowles's fiction. But the strongest definition of this theme of existential loneliness is made in the endings of the novels. Each ends in the isolation of the protagonist, but also in her or his self-awareness. Only *The Collector* has a closed, pessimistic ending, for Miranda is not allowed to enter the future. As in Poe's *The Cask of Amontillado,* the after image of *The Collector* is of a closed door, an airless walled-in cellar, which finally becomes a grave. Fowles's other novels, by contrast, provide open endings that are, in fact, not endings at all, but rather, new beginnings.

Both *The Magus* and *The French Lieutenant's Woman* end with essentially the same image: a man, alienated from a "new woman," standing isolated in the loneliness of selfhood.

Both novels end with the finding of a lost love. Both novels are circular. *The Magus* begins and ends with Alison, who serves as a catalyst for the formation of Nicholas's decisions. In the beginning, to escape human involvement with Alison, Nicholas takes the job on Phraxos and enters into his own selfhood. Symbolically, this existential development in Nicholas is represented by the two scenes, one near the beginning, the other near the end, that provide him with two opportunities to escape the loneliness of selfhood by committing suicide. Early in the novel Nicholas, planning to kill himself, hikes into the empty hills of Phraxos with a borrowed hunting rifle. On this occasion he fails to commit suicide out of simple indecision. He raises the gun and fires it "blindly into the sky" (58). Later in the novel, he finds himself in a similar situation. When he wakes up from his disintoxication, he is once again in a secluded place with a gun. This time, however, he decisively fires the six bullets out to sea and then hurls the gun after them. "It was *feu de joie*," he says, "a refusal to die" (482). By means of the godgame, he has developed the capability for making existential decisions.

Like *The Magus*, *The French Lieutenant's Woman* is also circular. It begins with Sarah Woodruff standing alone and lonely, gazing fixedly out to sea, and it ends with essentially the same scene, though in a different setting and with a new *isolato*. Charles Smithson replaces Sarah as he stands on the Chelsea embankment gazing out upon the Thames, the "river of life" that flows into "the unplumb'd, salt, estranging sea" (366). Like Nicholas Urfe, Charles has developed to the point where "he has at last found an atom of faith in himself, a true uniqueness, on which to build" (366). Thus, both novels move in a circle from loneliness to loneliness, and value lies in movement rather than in advancement. Just as Sisyphus always ends where he begins and yet finds value in his existence, so do Nicholas Urfe and Charles Smithson, though they do not progress out of loneliness, develop into selfhood. Movement into the self replaces movement forward in the superficial world.

The ending of *The Magus* is especially problematic. The last chapter begins with two spatial images. The first represents the situation of Fowles's hero who is "at a crossroads, in a dilemma, with all to lose and only more of the same to win," and the novelist is tempted to

> give him no direction, no reward; because we too are waiting, in our solitary rooms where the telephone never rings, waiting for this girl, this truth, this crystal of humanity, this reality lost through imagination, to return. (594)

This image defines Nicholas as a persona for modern man, who tries to find a way out of the enclaves of isolation, and who looks for exits from innumerable "waiting rooms." But, though tempted, Fowles cannot leave his hero alone in that closed room at the crossroads; the door must be opened and a road taken or not taken.

The second spatial image represents the very structure of *The Magus*, which tries, and fails, to deny the importance of an ending: "The maze has no center. An ending is no more than a point in sequence, a snip of the cutting shears" (594). Though Fowles tries to deny that his ending carries a higher charge of significance than any other part of his novel, though he tries to convince his reader that his novel-as-maze has no center, it doesn't work. The highly charged, symbolic ending that follows this "red herring" of a maze image shows Nicholas as changed from the man who stumbled, groped, and wandered blindly through the dark maze of the rest of the novel. Though perhaps not yet out of the maze, Nicholas, in the ending, has at least reached the center of the maze. He experiences the shock of recognition of who and where he is, and of what he must do to find his way out.

At one point in the ending Nicholas sees a blind man, "walking, freely, not like a blind man" (603). All men who live in the modern world, a world that has lost direction and from which God has disappeared, are blind men stumbling around in the dark. Some men are different, however: Even though blind, they walk freely; even though trapped, they still know where they are in the maze. In the ending of *The Magus* Fowles affirms the value of paradox and the necessity of absurd freedom: Though blind, a man must see; though lost, a man must be.

*The Magus* ends on All Hallows Eve and, significantly, as they confront each other, Nicholas and Alison are "unable to wear masks" (604). The fallen autumn leaves that color the ending scene suggest the paradoxical phoenix myth in which new life arises out of death. As Nicholas faces Alison he is aware of the "smell of a bonfire" (603) and as he walks away from her he feels "the stinging smell of burning leaves" (604). Throughout the scene the air is "as mellow as a harvest festival" (602). The autumn harvest brings death to nature's fruitfulness, but out of that death man finds the life that will sustain him through the winter. The seasonal imagery of the last chapter underlines the cyclical nature of *The Magus*. Nicholas has, indeed, passed through the fire of the godgame and will continue beyond the arbitrary snip of the shears of the novelist–god who ends the novel. This final confrontation with Alison is the ultimate disintoxication from the godgame, the burning away of all past falsehood, which is necessary before new existence can begin.

The seasonal imagery and the phoenix myth reinforce another familiar myth, that of the shamanic descent in which one dies in order to be reborn a magician, which is a dominant motif in *The Magus*. Nicholas had expected that Alison's reentry into his life would be another "metaphorical, perhaps even literal, descent into a modern Tartarus" (195). But when Alison finally reenters, it is as though "she had come from Tartarus" (596). The myth of descent into the underworld is fulfilled in the last chapter with images of resurrection, of return to reality from the mystery of another world. The autumn sky imitates "another world's spring" (594) and Kemp, the scruffy Virgil who leads Nicholas out of the underworld and into Regent's Park, seems "sent by hazard from a better world into mine" (595). Finally, Alison appears, trailing "the aura of another world" (596). Kemp has been paid by Conchis to lead Nicholas while Alison also has come from the world of the godgame, but the emphasis falls upon the separation of Nicholas from that other world. Nicholas must emerge from the underworld and take up a new life in the sunlight. The romantic revels now are ended and only the reality of life, "as plain and dull as wheat" (596), remains. From the godgame, however, it is hoped that Nicholas has taken the knowledge which will enable him to make bread, the stuff of existential life, from that dull wheat.

This scene of confrontation in Regent's Park is as important for Alison's future as it is for Nicholas's future. She too has been drawn into the godgame, and she too must be disintoxicated. In a sense, Nicholas has become a magus and is starting a new godgame replete with echoes of Conchis's masque. He places Alison in a dilemma of choice similar to that of Conchis standing in the town square with an empty gun before the *Eleutheria* man, or of himself standing with the cat in his hand before the soft, bare back of Lily. Alison must "choose, and choose for ever" (603), whether or not she will leave Conchis's godgame and join with Nick in his new lifegame. Ironically, just as Conchis's godgame began in the "SALLE D'ATTENTE," Nicholas and Alison's lifegame is scheduled to begin in the waiting room at Paddington Station. Whether this new beginning occurs or not, however, is matter only for conjecture because Alison's choice is made after the novel ends. What did happen at "Elsinore, that following spring?" (594). Perhaps the final words of the novel, the Latin epigraph, posit some hope that Nicholas and Alison will actually meet and learn to love each other in the future. It reads, "*cras amet qui numquam amavit quique amavit cras amet*": Tomorrow let him who has loved no one, love; whoever loves will tomorrow love.

Finally, the key to the ending of *The Magus* lies in the "row of white statues along the cornices [of] the aristocratic wall of houses that make up Cumberland Terrace" (597). Those statues represent, as the silent Christ figure does in Dostoevsky's *Legend of the Grand Inquisitor*, the "miracle, mystery and authority" of the godgame; the silent, aloof, merely observing God of the twentieth century, a god who has turned to stone and who no longer interferes in the business of men who must learn to make their own choices, live their own lives. Alison, come from another world, with her "smooth impermeability . . . like white marble" (599), also represents that god. The ending of *The Magus* was meant to be just as cryptic as "those white stone divinities" (602), those "pompous white pedimental figures" (604). The statues do, however, convey the message to Nicholas that the godgame is over and that he must learn to depend only upon himself if a new lifegame is to begin. And, as the magus of the new lifegame, knowing that Alison also must experience the loneliness of selfhood, Nicholas turns away from her with "a granite-hard face" (603).

Seemingly, the endings of *The French Lieutenant's Woman* ought to be more problematic than the ending of either *The Collector* or *The Magus* simply because there are more of them, three in all. But in reality, they are not. Compared to the cryptic mythic references and the symbolic representations of meaning in the ending of *The Magus*, the real ending of *The French Lieutenant's Woman*, the third and final one, is a straightforward statement of situation and theme. The final ending of *The French Lieutenant's Woman* is also much less problematic because it is so similar to the ending of *The Magus*.

The first ending of *The French Lieutenant's Woman* can be easily eliminated. If Fowles were intent only upon imitating the Victorian novel, Charles most plausibly might live out Chapter Forty-four's ending. After Ernestina "dewily" accepts Charles's gift and plants "a chaste kiss softly on his lips," the narrator intrudes upon the scene, which has grown, not pregnant, but obese with sentiment:

> It was simple: one lived by irony and sentiment, one observed convention. What might have been was one more subject for detached and ironic observation; as was what might be. One surrendered in other words; one learned to be what one was. (264)

This intrusion is couched completely in the past tense as a signal of its own impotency. Victorian novels traditionally conclude with scenes such as those in Chapter Forty-four. But, though imitating, Fowles is not writing a Victorian novel and thus, his metafiction simply cannot end so "dewily." Instead of this "thoroughly traditional ending" (266), he impels Charles Smithson into the same situation in which Nicholas Urfe earlier found himself. He places Charles in close "proximity of the moment of choice" and without "the benefit of existentialist terminology" Charles must face the loneliness of selfhood,

> the anxiety of freedom—that is, the realization that one *is* free and the realization that being free is a situation of terror. (267)

The first of the other two endings can also be eliminated for the same reasons that Fowles has eliminated Chapter Forty-four's Victorian ending. This ending in which Charles, Sarah, and the child, Lalage, are united and live happily ever after is just as sentimental as the previous Victorian ending. The ploy of a child uniting two alienated people is an antiexistential resolution that runs against the grain of Fowles's intentions as expressed in his own voice within this very novel. This ending denies both Charles and Sarah the power of choice and refuses to acknowledge the obstacles to their union built by their own clashing egos. All through the novel Sarah has been a stingingly, self-aware *isolato*, a seductive and destructive siren. Can she suddenly become a loving wife and mother? All through the novel Charles has been a hypocritically moralistic and pompous English gentleman. Can he suddenly rebel against centuries of convention? Can he have no suspicions whatsoever about the child's parentage? If these things could happen, then these characters would not be who they are. This ending is presented because Fowles does not want to deprive his mid-twentieth-century readers of their freedom of choice. In a novel based upon existential premises and in an existential world, people must be free to make inept choices as well as intelligent ones, and Fowles's readers certainly can choose the penultimate ending if they wish.

At the beginning of the last two endings of *The French Lieutenant's Woman*, as in the beginning of the ending of *The Magus*, Fowles attempts to deny the efficacy of all endings:

> The only way I can take no part in the fight is to show two versions of it. That leaves me with only one problem: I cannot give both versions at once, yet whichever is the second will seem, so strong is the tyranny of the last chapter, the final, the "real" version. (318)

Ostensibly, in order to nullify this "tyranny of the last chapter," Fowles presents the image of the coin toss that will decide the order of presentation of the two endings. As his image of the maze ushered in the ending of *The Magus*, this coin toss is also a "red herring" that attempts, and fails, to deny the precedence that the final (and only viable) ending of *The French Lieutenant's Woman* deserves. Though Fowles hasn't fixed the match in favor of one ending or another (only the individual reader, finally, can make that choice), this coin toss certainly is fixed. The reader never gets to see the coin, neither before nor after Fowles flips it. And, according to the dictates of either Fate or a two-headed coin, "the tyranny of the last chapter" conveniently falls to the most realistic, unsentimentalized ending.

The first character to appear in the last chapter of *The French Lieutenant's Woman* is the author himself, no longer "prophet-bearded" (316) but rather "foppish and Frenchified," a successful "impresario" (362). This new Fowles is much like Conchis, and the novel's world is "some new theater he has just bought" (362). Fowles, the "novelist–god," as does Conchis in *The Magus*, absconds in the last chapter from the godgame. Just as Conchis lures Nicholas deep into a heart of darkness, Charles Smithson is brought to "the end of his tether" (363), and as Charles stands completely alone on the Chelsea embankment, having rejected Sarah just as Nicholas rejected Alison, the god of the game turns the corner in his "trotting landau" (365) and passes out of sight.

Like the ending of *The Magus*, however, this final ending of *The French Lieutenant's Woman* is a new beginning. Phoenixlike, Charles feels as if he has "found himself reborn . . . all to be recommended, all to be learned again" (365). Like Nicholas Urfe staring at those white stone statues on the facade of Cumberland Terrace, Charles Smithson now realizes

> that there is no intervening god beyond whatever can be seen . . . thus only life as we have, within our hazard-given abilities, made it ourselves, life as Marx defined it—*the actions of men* (and of women) *in pursuit of their ends.* (365)

As an epigraph to the last chapter of *The French Lieutenant's Woman* Fowles quotes from Matthew Arnold's *Notebooks*: "True piety is *acting what one knows*" (361). And very near the end of the novel he comments on that epigraph: A "modern existentialist would no doubt substitute 'humanity' or 'authenticity' for 'piety'; but he would recognize Arnold's intent" (365–66). Marx, Arnold, the modern existentialist, all recognize and all affirm the loneliness of selfhood, and John Fowles dramatizes that isolation-in-identity in his spatial and mirror images, in the human situations of each of his novels, and especially in their open endings.